PROFILE OF A Cl

SERMONS ON THE BEATITUDES AND THE FRUIT OF THE SPIRIT

Graeme Stockdale

Foreword

For a few years now I have been self-publishing ebooks of sermon series preached during thirty or so years as a Baptist minister. A few months ago I decided to gather these together into one book ("Nourishment for Pilgrims"). I also decided to publish this as a paperback mainly for my own use. I was so pleased with the cost and quality of the book (produced by Amazon) that I am in the process of converting more of my Kindle books into paperbacks. There are certain parameters that have to be met and some of my ebooks are too short for publishing as paperbacks. I have therefore put two of them together in this book and hope that they will be of some use to the reader and fellow believer.

Graeme Stockdale
April 2022

THE BE-ATTITUDES

SERMONS BASED ON THE BEATITUDES

Graeme Stockdale

CONTENTS

Foreword

Chapter One
Blessed are the poor in spirit…

Chapter Two
Blessed are those who mourn…

Chapter Three
Blessed are the meek…

Chapter Four
Blessed are those who hunger and thirst for righteousness…

Chapter Five
Blessed are the merciful…

Chapter Six
Blessed are the pure in heart…

Chapter Seven
Blessed are the peacemakers…

Chapter Eight
Blessed are those who are persecuted for righteousness sake…

FOREWORD

The Beatitudes are a summary of the character profile of the follower of Jesus. They tend to be counter-cultural in terms of modern Western society but then this teaching has always been counter-cultural since the time these words were first spoken by Jesus. This book offers some thoughts on this important teaching, in the form of sermons preached over a period of thirty years or so.

I claim no originality for the title of this book and, despite searching, I have been unable to find the original source of this much used term for the Beatitudes. Nevertheless I have chosen the title because I have a feeling that the Beatitudes are more about 'being' than 'doing', about who we are rather than what we do.

As in my previous books of sermons, in common with many preachers I have gleaned ideas and sometimes phrases from a wide variety of sources – books, and of course, nowadays, the internet with its wealth of resources. At the time when the sermons were first written and delivered I did not make a note of sources. I do have a feeling, however, that the idea of the Christian being a revolutionary owes a great deal to a book written by the late Frank Cooke, formerly Senior Minister of Purley Baptist Church. I no longer possess this book and as far as I know it is no longer available. I will also have used some of William Barclay's teachings regarding the meaning of Greek words, together with various other commentaries.

I therefore wish to apologise to anyone reading this book who believes that I have made use of their resources without acknowledging the fact. If this is the case, please contact me so that I can at least include an acknowledgement in further updates.

And whilst taking into account my confession, if you are a preacher yourself, and wish to use any of the material in this book, for my part I am happy for you to do this without any acknowledgement, since I believe that these sermons, in truth, belong to God and not to me.

My prayer for you, the reader, is the prayer I have frequently prayed prior to preaching: that the Holy Spirit will inspire you in your reading and thinking so that you may be able to discern God's Word for you in the midst of human language.

Graeme Stockdale
February 2016

CHAPTER ONE

Blessed are the poor in spirit...

(Matthew 5:3)

I don't know if you've ever thought about it but those of us who stand at the front of churches week by week are not the only ones preaching sermons in today's world. As I talk with - young and old alike, children even - and as I listen to what they have to say, and as I watch television, and listen to the radio, or read newspapers, or simply observe the society in which we live, it becomes quite clear that we preachers are not the only ones trying to put across a message, or trying to influence people and shape their lives.

The world preaches its sermons millions of times each day, by every means possible, in words and pictures, actions and attitudes. Our 21st century world tells us our aims in life should be security, happiness, pleasure, health and wealth. We should be ambitious, we should seek personal satisfaction and fulfilment, we should even be ruthless and cunning in the pursuit of our goals, we should remain detached and not get too involved in anything in case we commit ourselves, and we should conform at all times, providing, of course it's the world's standards we're conforming to. This sermon is preached to and welcomed by young people, middle-aged people, and even the elderly. And it is important to realise this, that there are many voices in today's world, all endeavouring to influence us. If we don't realise this, then we will find it very difficult to grasp and appreciate the meaning, the implications and the challenge of the Sermon on the Mount, and the Beatitudes will be just fine-sounding but empty words as far as we are concerned.

But first, what do we mean by 'world'? If the 'world' shapes our thoughts and attitudes and actions, what do we mean by 'world'? Who are we referring to?

Schools have a huge influence on young lives. After all, teachers spend so much time with children and young people and during that time they can quite easily shape their thinking, their attitudes, their values, ideals, aims in life, for good or ill. But teachers quite rightly wouldn't accept all the responsibility for shaping these young lives. Parents, of course, play an important part, especially during the first five years of the child's life. By the time they start school, children already have a set of values and standards communicated to them by their parents.

Parents, in turn, point to other parents, or the influence of television, or DVDs or computer games as also having a major impact on their children's lives. When we are sitting round the table at my son's house and my grandson uses words most of us wouldn't even know how to spell, our daughter-in-law very quickly tells us he's picked it up from other children! This is, of course, quite possible. On the other hand, I recall Dr Colin Morris, the Methodist minister, speaking several years ago at a conference I attended. He pointed out that the five-year old at that time (the 1980s) was far more aware of the world in which we live than ever we were at five years of age. And the reason he gave was this – the child sits on the carpet in the living room, playing with his or her toys, and in the background all the time is the television, filling the child's mind with all kinds of things, some of them harmful, but also creating an awareness of the things that are happening in the world through the news media.

The media of television, radio, films and DVDs, newspapers and magazines also influence and shape the society in which we live. The media claim that they only *reflect* society, but they play a role in shaping society also by broadcasting what may initially be minority opinions or morals and values.

And so we could continue, pointing an accusing finger at

politicians, civil servants, industry, commerce, and so on, but the truth is that when we say 'world' we mean all of these influences including ourselves. Every one of us, to varying degrees, preaches and teaches by the things we do, the things we don't do, the attitudes and values we adopt, our behaviour, interests, priorities in life, enthusiasms and apathy. Every one of us is at the same time both teacher and pupil! Every one of us shares some of the responsibility for the society we live in, and if we are not happy with the way society is going, we have to ask ourselves: 'How can we change things? How can we change the direction of society?

The answer is that we need a revolution! Not a Marxist revolution, or a right-wing or left-wing revolution, or an uprising of anarchy. But we do need a revolution, and for this to happen, we need revolutionaries - people who are committed to changing the course of history, people who believe we can alter and shape the social and moral climate for future generations.

We need a revolution but all revolutions have to begin somewhere. And the one I have in mind begins inside each and every one of us, with a change of heart, a personal change that is the result of entering into a relationship with Jesus Christ as our Lord and Saviour.

The Sermon on the Mount is a guide, a handbook for revolutionaries, and it begins here in Matthew chapter five with a personality profile of a Christian revolutionary, otherwise known by the more familiar title, 'The Beatitudes' – an eight-fold description of this inner change that takes place when we commit our lives to Christ.

Many will be familiar with the passage in Galatians chapter five describing what we refer to as the 'fruit of the Spirit'. 'The fruit of the Spirit is love, joy, peace, patience, kindness, goodness etc'. One of my pet irritations is people referring to the fruits (plural) of the Spirit, as if the list of virtues was a menu, a list from which to choose. The suggestion by some people is that one fruit is 'love', another is 'joy', and so on. In Galatians chapter five, the apostle Paul is speaking (or writing) of one fruit, a composite picture of how a spirit-filled life should look, not a menu from which to make our selection. The same can be said of the Beatitudes. These eight qualities do not make up a menu. A menu is a list of options; the qualities and conditions listed in the Beatitudes are not options. These characteristics belong together, and together they give us a picture, a personality profile of a Christian revolutionary.

The first characteristic is found in Matthew 5:3 - **Blessed are the poor in spirit, for theirs is the kingdom of heaven.** The Good News Bible uses the word 'happy' instead of 'blessed' but nowadays the word 'happy' has become devalued and is not good enough for translating a word like this, not least because 'happy' has its roots in chance. William Barclay points out that the underlying Greek word does not describe an inner feeling, such as happiness, but a state of being, a condition. Barclay suggests that the word 'bliss' would be better – 'O the bliss of the poor in spirit…' - but 'Blessed' seems less clumsy.

Blessing means approval - we bless God when we express our approval of what he does, when we applaud him, when we praise and glorify him, presumptuous though this sounds! God blesses us when he graciously approves of us, our attitudes, or actions, or words.

Of course, the Bible teaches that even at our very best, **'all our righteousness is as filthy rags!'** There is certainly nothing we can do to earn salvation. Salvation and forgiveness and reconciliation with God come not through anything we can do, but are ours by the grace of God and the death of Christ. But God looks at us, and he reads our hearts, and measures our intentions and our sincerity, and, weak and inadequate though we may be, if our intentions and actions are in line with his will and purpose for us, God blesses us, he graciously gives us his approval. We don't win God's approval - God lovingly and graciously gives it. If we are genuinely poor in spirit, and hunger and thirst for righteousness, and are meek, pure in heart, peacemakers, and so on, God graciously gives his approval. This is the blessing God gives, and we shall return to this a little later. It is sufficient to say for now that this is a blessing no one can take from us, a blessing nothing can destroy.

Blessed are the poor in spirit... What does 'poor in spirit' mean?

This poverty is not the kind of poverty that is thrust upon some people by force of circumstance. This is not the kind of poverty, deprivation, suffering that is inflicted on some unfortunate and often helpless members of society, or on people who happen to have been born in the wrong part of the world, or even into the wrong families, people who find themselves in particular circumstances through 'accidents of birth' to use the language of Karl Marx. If it has anything at all to do with material poverty, it's the kind that is deliberately chosen or entered into.

Of itself poverty is not a virtue, nor is wealth a vice.

'Poor in spirit' here in Matthew's list of the Beatitudes refers to spiritual poverty. It's about recognising our need, knowing our limitations, acknowledging that our strength and our help are found in God, and God alone. Jesus is here teaching that material wellbeing is useless in the spiritual realm, that material things may preserve and protect us for a while, they may make us comfortable, but they are limited and confined to our time here on earth. Material things contribute nothing to our well-being in eternity.

So here is the first requirement for the Christian revolutionary, and it's to do with *being* rather than *doing*, who we *are* rather than what we *do*. Blessed are those who recognise their own weakness, helplessness, and realise that they lack those things that really matter in the spiritual realm. Blessed are those who let go of all that creates an illusion of security. Blessed are those who are willing to let go of things and take hold of God.

This beatitude comes at the head of the list as a reminder that God's blessing, God's approval is not given on account of our works, our efforts. The blessings promised here come in response to the transformation God works in us through the Holy Spirit. To be 'poor in spirit' is to depend utterly upon God and upon God's Spirit. Even our good intentions, our sincerity are the consequence of God's Spirit at work in our hearts and lives.

And what is the result of being 'poor in spirit'? Blessed are the poor in spirit **for theirs is the kingdom of heaven**. 'Kingdom of heaven' is just Matthew's Jewish way of saying Kingdom of God.

'… theirs is the Kingdom of God', not as a reward for good behaviour or sincerity of heart, but as a statement of fact.

It is interesting to note that this and the eighth Beatitude have the promise in the present tense; the other Beatitudes refer to a future promise. The Kingdom of God in all its fullness belongs to the future. There will be a time when Christ the King reigns in power and majesty, and no one will be in any doubt about it, but the Kingdom of God, the reign of God, is something we can enter into here and now.

And, it seems, we gain entry by having a humble spirit. Do you recall Jesus' words regarding children? **'I tell you the truth, unless you change and become like little children, you will never enter the kingdom of heaven.'** Jesus also said, **'Let the little children come to me, and do not hinder them, for the kingdom of heaven belongs to such as these.'** It may come as a surprise to us but according to Jesus, children are members, citizens of the Kingdom of God. This is why it is inappropriate to baptise children. It becomes appropriate later on in life because most, if not all, of us, rebel against God in some way or other as we grow and develop. But children as such already belong to the Kingdom of God, so we don't need to baptise them.

Children belong to God's kingdom, not because of a supposed innocence. Just ask any parent, or cast your mind back to when you were a child. Were you really all that innocent as a child? Children are members of God's kingdom because of their poverty of spirit. Children are not self-sufficient and they know it. On a daily basis the child is confronted with its own weakness, its need of help and attention. Day by day a child has to face the fact that there are some things it cannot do.

When a toddler shouts 'mum' from the smallest room in the house, that child is acknowledging its helplessness and dependence! When an 8 year old brings a broken toy to whoever looks after the Superglue in your house, it's a recognition of its helplessness. When your 12 year old comes home (as one of mine did once) asking 'How do you make a rain gauge?', it's an acknowledgement of helplessness (although it may also be a sign of the beginning of laziness!). Children are forced to admit that they can't do everything. In adolescence, of course, they may *know* everything and they may have an illusion of independence, but the truth is that they are still dependent.

What does Jesus say concerning these helpless creatures called children? He says **'theirs is the Kingdom of God'** And he says exactly the same with regard to the 'poor in spirit'.

Blessed are the poor in spirit, for theirs is the kingdom of heaven

What a contrast with the sermon preached by society! 'Blessed are those who are secure and self-sufficient, for they already have all they need!' 'Blessed are self-made people, blessed are the likes of Frank Sinatra – who did it 'their way'' But Jesus says, '**Blessed are the poor in spirit, for theirs is the kingdom of heaven**'.

Spiritual poverty is the first mark of the Christian revolutionary, showing dependence on nothing but the love, the grace and the power of God.

The words I use at just about every communion service I conduct seem to sum this up very well:

Come and share this bread and this wine, not because you must, but because you may.
Come not to testify that you are righteous, but that you sincerely love our Lord Jesus Christ
and desire to be his true disciple.
Come, not because you are strong, but because you are weak.
Come, not because you have any claim on heaven's rewards,
but because, in your frailty and sin, you stand
in constant need of heaven's mercy and help.

If you can echo these words sincerely and in your own heart of hearts say 'Amen', then rejoice, for the Kingdom of Heaven is yours!

Chapter Two

Blessed are those who mourn...

(Matthew 5: 4)

This man was driving along when suddenly he heard a police siren and saw a flashing blue light in his rear view mirror. The police car overtook him and the police officer signalled for him to pull in to the side of the road. The police officer then came towards the driver, so the man wound down the window and said, 'What's the problem officer?' 'Do you realise you were doing 75 miles an hour,' said the police officer. 'and the limit for this road is 50 miles an hour? I'm afraid I'm going to have to give you a speeding ticket.' 'Are you sure, officer?' said the man. 'I thought I was doing just a little over 50, if that.'

'Oh, Harry,' said his wife. 'You were doing at least 80!' The man gave his wife a look that spoke volumes.

'I'm also going to have to give you a ticket because one of your rear lights isn't working.' Said the policeman. 'I didn't know that.' Said the man. 'They were both working when I left home.'

'Oh, Harry,' said his wife. 'you've known about that rear light for weeks!' The man gave his wife another a dirty look.

'I'm also going to have to give you a ticket for not wearing your seat belt.' Said the police officer. 'But I only just took it off when I saw you coming towards me.' said Harry.

'Oh, Harry,' said his wife. 'you know you never wear your seat belt!' At this, the man turned to his wife and said, 'For goodness sake, can't you just keep quiet and let me handle this?'

The police officer turned to the woman and asked, 'Does your husband talk to you like this all the time?' 'Oh no, Officer, she said. 'Only when he's drunk.'

I am afraid that this has nothing to do with the reading from Matthew 5, or the Beatitude we are going to look at in this chapter, but they say laughter is good for us, and even if we can only manage a smile, then a smile is better than a frown!

Let's try another one –

A woman was giving her testimony in a church service and was talking about the tremendous change in her life following her conversion. 'For example,' she said. 'I have an uncle I used to hate so much that I vowed that I'd never go to his funeral. But now, I'd be happy to go to it!'

Or how about a story dating back to late 1940s in America? There was this family who lived in a remote part of the country and who were making their first visit to a big city. They checked in to a very expensive hotel and stood in amazement at the impressive surroundings. Leaving the reception desk, they came to the entrance to the lift, or as they would say, elevator. They'd never seen a lift before, and just stared at it, quite unable to work out what it was for. As they stood there an elderly lady hobbled towards the doors, the doors opened, she stepped inside, the door closed. About a minute later, the door opened again and out came a very attractive young lady. 'Son,' said Dad. 'Go and fetch your mother!'

The world loves to laugh! And many people earn a living from selling laughter and pleasure. Stand-up comedians are in some ways today's pop stars.

Ask people what their main aim in life is, and the reply is likely to be 'to have a good time', or something similar. The world does not like mournful people, miserable people, party-poopers, and I suspect that even Jesus himself had a great sense of humour and was fun to be with. I imagine the disciples had many a laugh together.

And yet what does Jesus say in the second Beatitude? **Blessed are those who mourn, for they will be comforted**

In the Beatitudes are a personality profile of a Christian revolutionary, then how does this idea that we need to be mournful fit in?

Let's take these familiar words and see if we can get behind them and understand a little of what Jesus was saying.

We need first of all to think about the word 'mourn'. What does it mean? In the original Greek the word used is a powerful word meaning the deepest of all sorrow, including sadness at the loss of a loved one, although in Greek there are also other words used to describe that kind of grief. Here the word is used of the sorrow, pain. anguish, torment of a broken heart.

A glance at the New Testament shows us that this word is not confined to mourning the death of someone close to us. For example, in 1 Corinthians 5:2, Paul has heard reports of gross misconduct in the church at Corinth and he says **'You are proud! Shouldn't you rather have been filled with grief...'** In 2 Corinthians 12:21, Paul writes of his fear that when he visits the church at Corinth he will grieve (mourn) over many who have sinned and not repented. In James 4:8-10, we read **'Come near to God and he will come near to you. Wash your hands, you sinners, and purify your hearts, you double-minded. Grieve, mourn and wail. Change your laughter to mourning and your joy to gloom. Humble yourselves before the Lord, and he will lift you up.'**

In each of these passages the word for 'mourn' (or 'grieve') is the word found here in Matthew 5:4, a word meaning, in general terms, 'broken hearted'.

Notice this though – this is not to say that we should be miserable all of the time. I am not saying that we should be like the person a little girl had in mind when she saw a horse and said, 'That horse must be a Christian - it's got such a long face!' This Beatitude gives no justification for that solemn, long-faced Christianity we sometimes encounter. The familiar passage in the Old Testament - Ecclesiastes 3 - says very clearly that there is a time to weep and a time to laugh; a time to mourn and a time to dance. So this Beatitude does not encourage our whole outlook on life to be miserable.

It's about personal grief. In the first place, personal grief over personal sin. Those who mourn are those who recognise first of all God's holiness and God's grace, and who then see the truth about themselves, and as a consequence are filled with deep remorse.

Psalm 51 is a psalm in which we are confronted with one man's intense grief. The context is David's adultery with Bathsheba, and the murder of her husband, Uriah the soldier, by ordering that he be placed on the front line in battle. The prophet Nathan comes to David and, through a parable, he challenges him concerning his sin. And in the words of Psalm 51 we catch a glimpse of David's grief, his mourning, his deep sorrow over what he has done. David cries out to God: **Have mercy on me, O God!** David is so convicted of his sin and so grief-stricken by it that he does not even make any personal claims on God. Notice that he does not address God as 'My God' but simply 'O God!'

This is a reminder that sin damages our personal relationship with God, and for David, it's this that breaks his heart. This isn't remorse in anticipation of judgement and punishment. This isn't David's concern at all. After all, Nathan has told him he will not die (which would have been the appropriate punishment for what he had done, according to the Law). David had been reassured regarding God's grace and mercy, but he was still broken-hearted. This grief, this mourning, this sorrow on account of his sin was not in anticipation of the punishment he might have expected or deserved, but it was rooted in a genuine remorse for what he had done – his personal grief at having sinned against God. His sin was not simply against Bathsheba or Uriah but against God himself. All sin is against God! David's broken heart cries out for mercy, for cleansing, for forgiveness.

This Beatitude is, in the first place, about personal grief over personal sin, and the acceptance of full responsibility for our own sin. Notice that David offered no excuses, no plea of mitigating circumstances, no apportioning of blame to others. He accepts personal responsibility for what he had done.

Moving on from David to the apostle Paul, we find a similar remorse. In 1 Timothy 1: 15 Paul writes: **'Christ Jesus came into the world to save sinners - of whom I am the worst.'** The 'worst of sinners, the chief of sinners…' I always see this as one of the few places where we can (and should) contradict the plain words of scripture! What do I mean? Well, if we were to compile a list of, say, the five worst people in history, the five most wicked, most evil people who ever lived, I don't imagine we would have even thought of including Paul in such a list. He did terrible things to first century Christians, but would Paul have been the first person who came to mind? And if, for some reason, his name was included on the list, and we then took a vote, do you really think the apostle Paul would come out at the top of the list? Do you really think Paul would qualify as the most wicked person who ever lived? I think not!

The point is this. When a person is genuinely deeply convicted of his or her own sin, and when that person has caught a glimpse of God's holiness and purity, then suddenly comparisons are meaningless as far as that person is concerned. In terms of sinfulness, others are of no concern. Paul was saying that as far as he was concerned, he himself was the worst of sinners. This is a sign of a broken and contrite heart.

In the first place then, this Beatitude is about personal grief over personal sin.

But it is also about those who grieve over the sins of the world, God's world, with all the dishonesty, the injustice, the greed, cruelty and violence, the selfishness.

At this point it would be very easy to go into a diatribe criticising the world and the way things are at the moment, criticising our own nation, and even our own local community. We could be critical of groups within the community, young people, so-called 'benefit scroungers', immigrants, mindless vandals and so on. Most of us are quite happy condemning anti-social behaviour, or people who don't fit in with our standards and values, but Jesus did not say *Blessed are those who condemn. . .* He said **Blessed are those who mourn** - those who care enough, feel deeply enough to weep and grieve. Sometimes we are content to walk with Jesus through Matthew 23 where he pronounces doom and gloom and speaks out in no uncertain terms against the hypocrisy of Pharisees. If we're honest we may even say that we enjoy all those 'Woes' against the religious leaders of his time. But how many of us are willing to stay with Jesus to the end of the chapter and stand there weeping with him as he looks over the city of Jerusalem and says: **O Jerusalem, Jerusalem. . . how often I have longed to gather your children together as a hen gathers her chicks under her wings, but you were not willing**

Blessed are those who don't just condemn the sins of the nation, but who grieve over society and the decline of moral values and social responsibility. Blessed are those who mourn over the fact that there are so few mourners!

This Beatitude then is about personal grief over sin - our own sin and the sins of world – a grief, a sadness, a deep sorrow, a heart that breaks when it sees sin for what it really is. And nowhere is the truth about sin revealed more clearly than at the foot of the cross of Christ. Have you ever stood there? We only need to use our imaginations and we can stand on the hill of Calvary and look, and see the results of those things we tend to excuse as just human weakness and failure. We can stand, and look, and ask 'Is that really what sin does?' Can sin really take someone as pure and perfect as Jesus and wilfully seek to destroy that perfection? Did <u>my</u> sin, does my sin, those failings I so readily dismiss, cause that?

The answer is 'Yes!'. The cross opens our eyes to show the horror of sin, the seriousness of sin, and the results of sin, and if we have an ounce of humanity, or sensitivity, then it should break our hearts.

But what does our text say? **Blessed are those who mourn, for they will be comforted**

To grieve, sorrow, mourn in this way is a great blessing, says Jesus! To have a broken heart is a blessing! And it is, because conviction of sin is the beginning of our journey towards forgiveness and liberation, salvation.

The comfort promised by God is not our usual idea of comfort - consolation, a sympathetic ear and kind words. Comfort here is about strengthening and renewal. God heals our broken-heart through Christ Jesus, and this comfort is the assurance of free and full forgiveness, and the knowledge that God does not reject us.

Returning to Psalm 51 again, even the broken-hearted David knew something of God's grace when he cried out, **Have mercy on me, O God, according to your unfailing love; according to your great compassion blot out my transgressions. Wash away all my iniquity and cleanse me from my sin.**

Society's message then is *aim to be happy*! Jesus'

message is **Blessed are the broken-hearted!**

The Jews were looking forward to the Messianic age, which was expected to be a time of gladness, rejoicing, festivity and happiness. And the Messiah came and said - **Blessed are the broken-hearted!**

Billy Graham once said – 'The happiest day of my life was when I realised that my own ability, my own goodness and my own morality were as nothing in the sight of God; and I openly acknowledged my need of Christ. I am not exaggerating when I say that my mourning was turned to joy, and my sighing into singing.'

Today could be the happiest day in **your** life, the happiest day so far… but it has to begin with a broken heart!

Chapter Three

Blessed are the meek…

(Matthew 5: 5)

Here in the United Kingdom we have a democratic system of government. Democracy is not perfect but it seems to be the best form of government for a modern nation. Democracy, of course, involves holding elections from time to time to decide who will represent us in the House of Commons, or in local government. Voting in a democracy such as ours is, I believe, a great and hard-won privilege. I am saddened therefore by a widespread apathy among those entitled to vote, not least because such apathy can allow extremist parties to gain power.

Assuming, however, that we are not infected with this apathy, I wonder what sort of things influence us most when we cast our vote. We may be influenced mainly by party loyalty, or by particular policies, or the failure of past policies, or just the way a person looks and speaks.

One thing I am certain of is that very few people are be influenced by whether or not the candidate has described himself or herself as being 'meek'! Even those seeking election who profess to be Christians do not major on meekness in their campaign literature. After all, people want someone who will speak up for them, someone to represent them, someone to stand up for them, not someone who wouldn't say 'boo to a goose!', or as someone put it, someone so unsure of himself that he could be pushed over by a hard slap from a wet noodle!

On several occasions when I have attended the Baptist Assembly in London, I have taken the opportunity to go to the public gallery of the House of Commons. I have usually managed to identify some famous faces, but the rest of the Members of Parliament present were unknown to me. I do know this one thing about them thought. I would be willing to guess that not one of those MPs was elected on account of his or her meekness. The same would be true, I'm sure, of those in positions of leadership in all walks of life - in industry, trades unions, education, local government, and even in the church! I wonder if 'meekness' has ever appeared on a church profile when that church was looking for a new minister!

Meekness is not usually a quality applauded by society in general, and it never was, and yet when Jesus set out the Beatitudes, this character profile of a Christian revolutionary, he said, among other things: **Blessed are the meek, for they shall inherit the earth**

On this occasion we are not going to look at the second half of this verse - '**inherit the earth**' - because I think this is just a promise for the future, an encouragement for those who are prepared to forego this world's riches in order to cultivate something more important and of greater value. I think, therefore, that Jesus is just saying that the rich and powerful, who think that the earth and everything in it is theirs, are in for a bit of a shock! The Bible says **The earth is the Lord's and everything in it** and it's God's to give to whomever he chooses, and God chooses to give his inheritance to the meek, to those who least expect it.

Let's focus on the first half of this Beatitude because I think there is plenty for us to think about here in these words alone - **Blessed are the meek**

I wonder what images this word **'meek'** conjures up?

There was this rather timid and submissive wife who wanted to impress her feminist friend, so she said... 'My husband and I are completely equal in the sight of God and I can assure you that I have my husband's full permission to say so!' Is this a picture of meekness? Or perhaps the hen-pecked husband? There was once a young husband was so henpecked that he decided to go to a psychiatrist to help him with the problem. The psychiatrist told him, 'You don't have to put up with this! You don't have to let your wife bully you! Go home and show her you're the boss!' So the young man went home, slammed the door, slammed his fist on the table and said, 'From now on, woman, you're taking orders from me! When I get home from work, I want my supper on the table. I want my clothes laid out ready for me each day. I will be going out with the lads on Friday nights. You will be staying home. And another thing. Do you know who's going to tie my tie and brush my hair?' 'Yes' she said: 'The undertaker!' Is this what it means to be meek? Does this word 'meek' mean 'weak'?

The dictionary definition seems to suggest this. Meek means 'tamely submissive' and this is certainly in line with modern usage. Meekness describes those who seem to be walked upon, trampled underfoot, taken advantage of, manipulated, exploited. But is this what Jesus has in mind?

Well, ironically the answer is yes and no, which sounds like a bit of a meek answer! On the face of it, the meek have a raw deal in life, a rough time, but the strange thing is that, in reality, the meek person is in control! The meek person is the strong person.

Christianity is full of paradoxes and here's one: the one who allows himself or herself to be pushed around is the one who is really in control! And far from being weak, that person is strong.

The late Frank Cooke, a Baptist minister, says that meekness is to do with taking hold of the cave-man within us and harnessing all that animal energy to constructive ends. Whenever I think of meekness in these terms my mind goes back to the days when I was a child and much of my time before I started school and during school holidays was spent on a local farm, near where we lived, on a council estate three miles north of Nottingham. My parents were friendly with the farmer and his wife, so I was allowed to spend a lot of time on the farm. There was a carthorse there called Rascal, a good natured. gentle, loveable animal. I often rode on his back, even as a 5, 6, 7 year old. There was another carthorse called Dandy but I was never quite so sure and confident with him. Rascal and I were great friends though. I've seen him pull milk carts, drays stacked with milk crates and churns, up hills and down hills. I've seen him pull the plough across fields. I've seen him do all the things a working horse did in those days. He had immense strength, but at the same time a gentle strength, controlled strength. Perhaps Rascal (and maybe even Dandy) can teach us something about the true meaning of meekness.

In fact, the Greek word used here can be used of domesticated animals. Of course, horses need to be broken in before all that power can be harnessed and used, (and perhaps this says something to us too), but what did my dictionary say? 'tamely submissive' - perhaps there is an element of truth in this definition of meekness after all. Or would we prefer Bible commentator Donald Carson's definition? 'Meekness is a controlled desire to see other's interests advance ahead of our own.'

Whatever we say, one thing is certain. We must not equate meekness and weakness. Meekness demands strength, self-control, discipline. We are meek when we suffer wrong without bitterness, when we endure adversity and opposition without a desire for revenge or retaliation, when we forego what we are entitled to, when we surrender our rights and interests rather than spend our time safeguarding them.

Let me offer two examples of meekness from the Old Testament.

In Genesis 13 we read about Abram and his nephew Lot. Both had flocks and herds, sheep and cattle, but we read that **the land could not support them while they stayed together... and quarrelling arose between Abram's herdsmen and the herdsmen of Lot. . . so Abram said**

to Lot 'We can' t have all this quarrelling between us. Let's separate and you choose which way you'll go.'

Lot looked out over the whole of the countryside and saw that the plain of Jordan was well-watered, so he chose to go that way, and Abram, who could have claimed seniority and therefore could have had the first choice, settled for inferior pasture land and allowed Lot the first choice. That was meekness on Abram's part. Meekness, not weakness.

In Isaiah 53 we find another description of meekness. **Surely he took up our infirmities and carried our sorrows, yet we considered him stricken by God, smitten by him, and afflicted. But he was pierced for our transgressions, he was crushed for our iniquities; the punishment that brought us peace was upon him, and by his wounds we are healed. We all, like sheep, have gone astray, each of us has turned to his own way; and the Lord has laid on him the iniquity of us all. He was oppressed and afflicted, yet he did not open his mouth; he was led like a lamb to the slaughter, and as a sheep before her shearers is silent, so he did not open his mouth.** There we have another example of meekness. Meekness, not weakness.

Jesus says meekness is meant to be one of characteristics of his disciples - not of *some* of his disciples but of all of them! And this quality is commended in the rest of the New Testament. In 2 Corinthians 10: 1 Paul appeals to the Corinthian Christians **by the meekness and gentleness of Christ.** In describing the fruit of the Spirit in Galatians 5:22, 23 Paul includes meekness (NIV 'gentleness') In Colossians 3:12 we read **clothe yourselves with compassion, kindness, humility, meekness and patience.** In 1 Peter 3: 15f - **Always be prepared to give an answer to everyone who asks you to give the reason for the hope that you have. But do this with gentleness (meekness) and respect.** And in James 1:21 we read, **Get rid of all moral filth and the evil that is so prevalent, and humbly (meekly) accept**

the word planted in you, which can save you. There
are eleven other New Testament references to meekness.

Clearly the New Testament writers were not afraid to
commend meekness as a Christian virtue. so how come
we think so little of the word? The simple answer is that
our attitudes are influenced more than we care to admit
by the grabbing, self-asserting materialism of the world,
which has infected our lives! What's to be done then?
How can we appreciate and cultivate this quality?

First of all we need to understand that the Beatitudes are
not commands. We are not here commanded to be meek.
Meekness is a gift from God, part of the fruit of the Holy
Spirit. We can really only possess this quality by the
grace of God and through the working of the Holy Spirit
in our hearts. But having said this, we can help, not least
by co-operating with the Holy Spirit.

What is the opposite of meekness? Arrogance, pride,
self-assertiveness, standing up for our rights, making
sure we get everything we consider to be due to us. And
if we don't have the confidence to stand up for our own
rights then the opposite of meekness is seen in
harbouring resentment, bitterness, pain when we feel our
rights have been overlooked or denied us, inner pride and
anger.

I suspect that all of these have their roots in a basic
insecurity, a need to have some identity, a need to have
people respect us and recognise us for who we are and
what we have done, or perhaps who we like to think we
are. When we get angry, resentful, bitter, it is often
because we feel misunderstood, mistreated, misjudged,
unappreciated, and somewhere in all this is a sense of
uncertainty, of insecurity.

We can really only be meek when we are secure, when
we know who we are, especially in relation to God, when
we have found our true identity in Christ.

In Psalm 8 the Psalmist asks **'What is man?'** The philosopher and scientist may join together and present a picture of man as a 'cosmic orphan', alone and lost, an insignificant speck in a vast, hostile universe. No wonder we feel insecure! But Christ points us to a heavenly Father and gives us a family. When know God as our Father we can afford to be meek, to be walked over and even pushed around.

Meekness, like so many Christian virtues, finds its source and strength in a correct understanding of God and our relationship with him. It begins with a belief in the infinite goodness and greatness of God, in his sovereignty, his wisdom, his holiness, his loving kindness, his faithfulness, and righteousness. It begins with the recognition of God also as one who gives and gives and who goes on giving. It begins when we realise we can trust God and go on trusting him regardless of circumstances.

Martin Lloyd Jones says that meekness is about leaving everything to God, ourselves, our rights, our cause, our whole future - everything in the hands of God, especially if we feel we are suffering unjustly!

This is what the Psalmist says in Psalm 37 - **Be still and know that I am God**

That's meekness! A confidence in God that allows us to 'be still'. to be exposed to our enemies, whatever form they may take, and yet not be fearful, discontented, rebellious, resentful, but rather be quiet, patient, cheerful, even in face of adversity.

Meekness comes from knowing who we are, and *being* who we are: sons and daughters of the Living God! You and I will never be meek if we do not know who we are.

As always Jesus provides the supreme example. He is the one described in those verses in Isaiah 53. He is the one who made no complaint, in whom no bitterness, or desire for revenge was found in return for the abuse he suffered. Jesus did not stand up for his own rights even though he could have called upon millions of angels to rescue him from the cross. Instead he used his voice to speak words of forgiveness and grace.

Meekness is desperately needed these days, not only in the world around us, but in our churches too. Why? Because meekness earths anger, jealousy, resentment, hatred, bitterness and negativity. I am sure we all know what a lightning conductor does. It offers a measure of protection during a thunderstorm by earthing electrical charges in the atmosphere before they can do damage. Meekness acts like a lightning conductor, earthing evil in all its forms before it can do irreparable damage.

In Romans 12 Paul says **Do not repay evil with evil.** Don't bounce it around, but kill it dead!

The cross of Christ is not just a symbol of sacrificial love. The cross is also a vivid picture of meekness - meekness that faces up to abuse and violence and hatred and earths it all, taking away its power to cause damage.

Blessed are the meek, for they shall inherit the earth

It isn't easy when the world is bombarding us with its values. No one would pretend that it is, which is precisely why we need to ask God to give us this essential Christian quality – meekness.

Chapter Four

> Blessed are those who hunger and thirst for righteousness...
>
> (Matthew 5:6)

We only have to glance at the television, or browse through the newspapers and glossy magazines, looking especially at the advertisements, and it becomes clear that, to be successful in life, we have to know how to satisfy our appetites, what to ask for, how to ask for it, and knowing what's 'in' and what's 'out'. The successful person by today's standards drives the right model of car, owns a house in the right school catchment area, is climbing a career ladder, buys the right clothes, from the right shop – online or in the High Street, and judges others by the standard of his or her own success. In other words, the successful person knows how to satisfy his or her appetites, and fill life with all kinds of good things.

And those who can't keep up in the race of life are left feeling useless, inadequate, a complete failure!

The successful man or woman of the twenty first century therefore can be said to hunger and thirst for fulfilment, satisfaction and the knowledge of being right up there with the leaders, the winners of society.

It is interesting that there is nothing new about this. The Jews at the time of Jesus were also hungry and thirsty. They longed for the coming of the Messiah and his Kingdom. They were desperately looking and longing for deliverance from their Roman oppressors. But this wasn't their only reason for longing for the Messianic Kingdom. They also desired wealth and honour and dignity and respect and dominion, power over all the nations of the world as a sign of God's blessing upon them.

But Jesus said: 'I'm sorry to disappoint you. Those who

seek such things will not be filled. **Blessed are those who hunger and thirst for righteousness: for they will be filled.**

Now, there is one thing we have to recognise as we read the gospel accounts of the life and teaching of Jesus. It is quite obvious that, in many ways, there is an enormous gap between the times of Jesus and our own times. Their situation was very different from ours. And in order to understand the fourth Beatitude, we have to recognise this, because if we don't, then the Word of God here will lose its impact.

Blessed are those who hunger and thirst for righteousness: for they will be filled

The problem today is that we don't really know what real hunger and real thirst are. I know that millions of people in today's world **do** know these experiences. Through the mass media and through the promotional material and appeals of charities and missionary organisations, we are aware of the plight of so many people in so many parts of the world, right up to our doorstep with the shameful current need for foodbanks in our own country.

Millions today hunger and thirst for physical food, basic sustenance to keep them alive from one day to the next, while most of us in the Western world are spoilt and sometimes bewildered by the choice of food in our supermarkets.

In one of the churches where I served as minister, we had monthly 'frugal lunches' to remind us of the needs of others, whilst at the same time raising money for various worthy charities. We usually had just bread and cheese, but simple bread and cheese would be regarded as a banquet compared with what many people have to make do with daily.

We don't really know what real hunger is!

In Palestine, at the time of Jesus, the daily wage was about 1p or 2p. Even if we adjust this for real purchasing power today, I'm sure we would agree that you aren't likely to have a problem with obesity 1p or 2p per day, especially when it had to feed a family. In the days of Jesus, an average family ate meat perhaps once a week, and a working man, a day labourer and his family were never very far from starvation. Hunger - real hunger – was very much within their experience.

I suppose thirst might be closer to our experience. I suspect we have all experienced thirst, especially on a hot summer's day. For example, perhaps you are out for a walk in the countryside, miles from anywhere, and suddenly you have an intense longing for something to drink. The longing, the thirst becomes even more intense, especially if you have exhausted your supply of water and you know you can't have anything to drink.

I remember a school trip when I was about 12 years old. We went from Nottingham to London by train, to visit the Planetarium and Madame Tussauds. Trains were slow in those days; the journey was probably about three hours or so, and there were no air-conditioned carriages. We hadn't even heard of air-conditioning! We also weren't quite so *au fait* with the need to stay hydrated and make sure we had plenty of drinks. I recall that the train was stuffy and hot and I was very thirsty. The teachers had some lukewarm tea left, just tea with no milk or sugar. But I remember that my thirst was such that I was very glad of that cup of tea they gave me!

Most of us have some idea of what it means to be thirsty. The difference between us and the Jews of Jesus' day is that we can usually find some way of quenching our thirst. In Palestine there were no taps, no ready supply of cool, clear water. Even today drinking water is at a premium in the Middle East.

Travellers in that part of the world tell of sandstorms and scorching winds, and of the mouth and throat becoming so parched that they feel that they are going to suffocate. I am sure very few of us have experienced quite such an intensity of thirst.

Blessed are those who hunger and thirst for righteousness – Blessed are those who have such an intense longing, yearning **for righteousness** that it feels like a matter of life and death! Not only have few, if any, of us experienced this kind of physical hunger and thirst, but I suspect that few of us have also had this intense longing for righteousness.

This word 'righteousness' is often equated with the narrow-minded prudishness of Victorians. Today Christians may desire maturity, and real joy and happiness; some seek the Spirit's power in life, some desire greater witnessing skills, others long for meaningful worship. Some go from church to church, preacher to preacher, conference to conference in search of these things, as they hunger and thirst for some spiritual experience, some emotional lift, to keep them going in their journey of faith. But how many seek righteousness?

I am not saying that these other things are not important, but I don't see them listed here in the Beatitudes, these verses, these teachings of Jesus about the basics of Christian discipleship. But I do see this… **Blessed are those who hunger and thirst for righteousness: for they will be filled.**

Martin Lloyd Jones says… 'I do not know of a better test that anyone can apply to himself or herself in this whole matter of the Christian profession than a verse like this. If this verse is to you one of the most blessed statements of the whole of Scripture then you can be quite certain you are a Christian; if it is not, then you had better examine the foundations again.'

But what does it mean – 'righteousness'? Unfortunately, this word defies simple definition. It has been described as being a 'vast and complex concept'. 'Righteousness' is a word used to describe God's behaviour towards us and our behaviour towards God. In essence 'righteousness' means doing the right thing. It is a covenant word and refers to the fulfilling of the obligations of the covenant partners, maintaining the conditions of a contract, keeping our side of the bargain.

God is righteous in that he always does what is right, fulfilling his promises, keeping his word, always acting in our very best interests. For our part, righteousness describes a pattern of life which conforms to the will of God, and again is about doing the right thing by doing what God requires of us.

It has been said that righteousness is not about drifting aimlessly in a sea of empty religiosity but is far more positive than this. Nor is it to do with pottering about pursuing trivial and inconsequential distractions. An understanding of the nature of human righteousness is perhaps more accurately reflected in the prayer of a Scottish Christian – 'O Lord, make me as holy as a pardoned sinner can be!'

Righteousness then is a pattern of life conforming to the will of God, and it begins with a deep longing for a right relationship with God. If for you God is no more than an impersonal force, some hostile and indifferent being, some useful explanation of the mysteries of creation and no more, or if you see God almost as an enemy, intent on catching us out, watching for us to do something wrong, looking for excuse to punish us, or if words like 'Father', and 'friend', 'Helper', are not words you would use to describe God, then let me suggest that you do not have a right relationship with God.

In the Lord's Prayer, Christ encourages us, instructs us to address God as 'our Father'. Christ died in order to make it possible for us to approach the Father free from the guilt and taint of sin. His sacrifice on the cross opened up a new and living way for us to draw near to God, and to know the reality of what it means for God to be our Father and we his sons and daughters. We have fellowship with God through the sacrificial death of Christ, which we appropriate for ourselves through faith - faith which leads us first of all to repent of our sinful way of life (which simply means a way of life which excludes God). Faith allows us to recognise that we are saved not by any amount of works on our part but by the grace of God. Faith leads us to trust in God, and in God's way of living shown in Jesus.

If we earnestly desire a right relationship with God, there are four things we need to do:

(i) **Confess** our spiritual need, which means acknowledging to God that we have not been living in his way; we have not been giving him first place in our lives;

(ii) **Repent**. It is an old-fashioned word and it simply means 'about turn! Repentance is about making a decision to turn around, and follow a new direction in life. It means, instead of walking away from God, turn around and start walking towards him;

(iii) **Believe** that Jesus died for us on the cross.. It does not mean that we have to understand all that this means but we need to believe and begin to live life on the basis of our belief;

(iv) **Receive** – we need to welcome Jesus Christ into our hearts and lives, welcoming him as Lord and Saviour

Confess, Repent, Believe, Receive – we can do this right now, even as I continue to speak, or we can do it by finding a quiet space at home, or we might prefer to have someone to help us. The important thing is to respond to Christ's invitation and begin experiencing this relationship with God as our Father.

But not only is righteousness about having a right

relationship with God. It is also about having a right relationship with one another, and this in itself opens up a whole new range of subjects.

For example, to hunger and thirst for righteousness may mean a deep longing for social justice. In Isaiah 56:1 we read: **This is what the Lord says: 'Maintain justice and do what is right for my salvation is at hand and my righteousness will soon be revealed.'** Such a hunger and thirst is costly for Christians in many parts of the world and the cost may be a person's life, or the loss of freedom, peace, human dignity, liberation.

To hunger and thirst for righteousness may mean an earnest desire for reconciliation and a willingness to be involved in building bridges across divides in our nation, in the wider world, or in our local community, or even between churches, and in our churches.

Jesus promises that those who have a deep longing to pursue the will and purposes of God will be filled. If we long to live a life conformed to the will of God, and if our longing is enough to find expression in practical action, then our hunger and thirst will be satisfied. This does not mean that everything we do will be successful, but we will have the blessing and joy of sharing God's concerns, and pursuing his agenda. After all, when we align our lives with the will of God, how can God do anything else but bless us?

Blessed are those who hunger and thirst for righteousness: for they will be filled

This is not about superficial hunger and thirst, but a deep hunger of soul. So, I believe we are left with a question and a challenge. How much do you long for this righteousness? How much do you desire to be right with God? How much do you want to be walking with God? As much as a starving African longs for some morsel of food? As much as a parched throat in a desert storm longs for water?

So the question comes with a built-in challenge - *How much do you hunger and thirst for righteousness?*

But there is not only a challenge here but a note of encouragement too. The question doesn't ask 'How **good** are you? How **righteous** are you? Jesus is not even saying 'Blessed are those who **are** righteous.' He is saying 'Blessed are you, even though you have not yet achieved perfection! Blessed is the one who, in spite of failure, still reaches for perfection; still strives for the highest. Blessed is the one who doesn't hide behind the excuse of human frailty.'

Blessed are those who hunger and thirst for righteousness: for they will be filled.

Chapter Five

Blessed are the merciful…

(Matthew 5:7)

Jesus said: Blessed are the merciful, for they will be shown mercy. But it just isn't true, is it? There we were playing in a 5 a side football tournament and we actually made it to the final. There we were, doing our best to be meek and merciful, and did the other team show any mercy? It just is not true - **Blessed are the merciful, for they will be shown mercy.** Or perhaps, if we're honest, we were not as meek and merciful as we would like to think. Perhaps that was just an excuse, and maybe we were just not quite good enough to lift the trophy! I'm not sure we could have managed enough energy to lift the trophy anyway, after playing five games in less than 4 hrs.

Each year our church held a Spotlight on Sport weekend, beginning with a Sports Supper, with food, invited guests and usually a sports chaplain as speaker. And then on the Saturday we would have more than fifty people from various churches and organisations taking part in the five-a-side football tournament, and the guest speaker would speak again at our Sunday morning service.

I believe that Jesus would have loved a Sports Weekend in his day. I believe he would have taken an interest in sport, because it offers a great opportunity for getting alongside of people and building relationships. But I'm not sure Jesus actually had competitive sport in mind when spoke the words we're looking in this chapter! **Blessed are the merciful, for they will be shown mercy**

Picture the scene. A great and powerful king is seated on his throne and at his feet is a miserable wretch, on his knees, his hands clasped together, begging, pleading for **mercy**. Or perhaps we might think of a law court where the sentence is about to be passed and the counsel for the defence puts in a plea for **mercy.** In these contexts what does mercy mean? Leniency?

Think too of other contexts, other ways in which this word, 'mercy' might be used. For examples, we speak of acts of mercy, and we think of people like Mother Teresa and many others, engaged in acts of **mercy** on the streets of Calcutta and in many other places around the world. We think of those working tirelessly to relieve suffering and deprivation in so many parts of world, performing acts of mercy.

Or we might think of euthanasia, assisted dying. Not everyone will agree with me but I believe euthanasia to be wrong and contrary to God's will. Having said this, I would not deny that many of those who advocate euthanasia do so as an act of mercy for those suffering terrible and distressing conditions. So we speak of 'mercy-killing', killing with kindness, and I would be among the first to say that most of time euthanasia is carried out for compassionate reasons.

Mercy then can also mean kindness. In terms of justice and guilt, mercy means leniency. In terms of suffering, it means compassion, kindness. So when Jesus says **Blessed are the merciful, for they will be shown mercy**, which does he mean?

I see no reason why he can't both leniency and kindness. In terms of human misery and suffering, the merciful person is someone who opposes cruelty and injustice, and also someone who seeks to relieve or prevent misery and suffering.

This whole idea of mercy was not universally welcomed in Jesus' day. As far as the Greeks were concerned, mercy was simply an emotion aroused by the suffering of others and although it was looked upon as a virtue by some, it was also regarded as a sickness by others!

The Romans did not show very much by way of mercy, especially in the lands they occupied. Roman society had a very harsh, cruel, sadistic element.

Even the Jews did not show much mercy for a particular reason. They understood suffering to be the result of sin. The person who suffered must have done something to deserve it. Suffering was God's punishment, so to show mercy would be to intervene in an act of God. It would be tantamount to interfering and meddling with God's judgement on that person.

This whole idea of mercy was not universally welcomed in Jesus' day, so what happened? Along came Jesus and turned people's thinking upside down! For the Greeks, mercy was an emotion, a sickness, but Jesus talks about mercy being love, compassion, pity in action. **Blessed are the merciful** - blessed are those who have compassion on those in need, those who see people in their helplessness and hopelessness and misery, and are moved to do something. Blessed are those who look upon others less fortunate than themselves, and who treat them with understanding and dignity and gentleness, and who work to bring comfort and relief.

Now, whether we think of mercy in terms of leniency, or as a response to suffering and misery, there is a common element. In both cases we are speaking about a disparity, an inequality, and the common element is this. Mercy, like liquids, always flows downwards, from strength to weakness.

In George Orwell's book, 'Animal Farm' we have the famous quotation - 'all animals are equal but some animals are more equal than others!' It is a contradiction in terms, of course but we can say this: *All people equal but not all circumstances are equal.* Some people are privileged while others live in poverty and deprivation. Some people are the 'haves, while others are the 'have-nots'. This word 'mercy' describes the flow of compassion from those who 'have' to those who 'have-not', from the strong and privileged to those who are weak, vulnerable and deprived.

Mercy is the downward flow of love, and compassion and pity, and it is an attitude not merely commended by Jesus, but required of every Christian disciple, every Christian revolutionary.

Note, however, that there are two sides to this coin called 'mercy'.

Blessed are the merciful... why? Why are the merciful blessed? Why are they so fortunate? Why is their condition described as 'bliss'? The answer is: ...**for they will be shown mercy,** because they are promised mercy, they will themselves be blessed with mercy.

These words would have come as something of a shock to those Jewish hearers of the first century. The traditional Jewish view was that those who hated evil and sin would be blessed, those who sought to eradicate evil and who sought vengeance on God's behalf would be blessed. And the blessing would be seen in terms of power, wealth, and material possessions. But Jesus speaks of mercy and commends the merciful, and promises not material wealth and power but mercy itself!

This puts us in our place, doesn't it? If mercy always flows downhill, then it puts us firmly in our place! On the one hand we are called to be merciful, to recognise our strength and privilege, and to exercise ourselves in the relief of suffering, but at the same time we are reminded of our own need, poverty and weakness, and perhaps even guilt.

It is a humbling experience to come to terms with the fact that every one of us is in need of mercy. It is a sobering thought to identify ourselves in words I tend to use at services of Holy Communion - *in our frailty and sin we stand in constant need of heaven's mercy and help.*

Words like 'guilt' and misery' have already been mentioned. God responded to our guilt by his grace, his love poured out to those who don't deserve it. God's Word and God's Spirit condemn us as rebels, sinners standing in need of grace and forgiveness, and by the grace of God in Jesus Christ we can be forgiven.

Grace goes with guilt - it's God's response to our sinfulness - but mercy takes it further. God in his mercy looks at us and sees us as those who bear marks of sin, the scars of our own folly, the results of our wrongdoing. He sees our pitiful state, and that we are in desperate need of help, and in a great act of mercy God sends his Holy Spirit. The Spirit of God comes into the centre of our lives to renew us, heal us, transform us and help us to be the people God would have us to be. The coming of the Holy Spirit on the Day of Pentecost was itself an act of divine mercy.

God is, by his very nature, a merciful God. A tax collector comes to the temple to pray. He comes full of shame and remorse and despair, and he stands in the shadows and cries out: **God, have mercy on me. a sinner**. And in this parable this tax collector discovers that God is indeed merciful – full of mercy. The Psalmist reminds us: **God does not treat us as our sins deserve or repay us according to our iniquities** and it is true, isn't it? **God does not treat us as our sins deserve or repay us according to our iniquities**

Every one of us, without exception, has been blessed with God's mercy already, and the promise is that God will bless us again. But it is two-way traffic, as is so often the case with God.

Jesus said that we should pray **Forgive us our sins as we forgive those who sin against us.** Why should we forgive? Because we ourselves have been forgiven and we continue to seek forgiveness from God. Why should we be merciful? Because of God's great mercy towards us already, and because we continue to need his mercy day by day. And to what extent will God forgive us? It seems to have something to do with our own willingness to forgive others. To what extent will God show mercy towards us? It seems to be according to our own willingness to exercise mercy.

Jesus taught this in several parables. In the parable of the Rich Man and Lazarus, the rich man is condemned and denied mercy. Why? Because he had not shown mercy when the opportunity presented itself daily on his doorstep in the shape of Lazarus. In Matthew 25 we have the picture of the sheep and goats, and Jesus says that people will be separated into two groups just as a shepherd separates the sheep from the goats. One group, he says, will sent into the eternal fire prepared for the devil and his angels. The other group will be invited to share in God's kingdom. What distinguishes the two groups from each other? Acts of mercy - feeding the hungry, clothing the naked, welcoming the stranger, visiting the prisoner, taking care of the sick. It's about how we respond to those in need, and Jesus says that our response should include mercy shown in practical ways.

Blessed are the merciful. for they will be shown mercy

We and all followers of Christ been given an errand of mercy. We are sent to witness, to serve the community around us, and in so doing we are sent to minister to the whole person, body, mind and spirit. But where do we begin? How do we develop this characteristic in our own lives?

It begins with a proper respect for all people. It begins with a belief in human dignity and the value of the individual. It begins in seeing men and women through God's eyes, and not through the cloudy cataracts of our own prejudices.

It begins with a proper respect for all people, and then

moves on to seeing the world through other people's eyes, especially through the eyes of those who suffer, those who are weak and vulnerable, the poor, the sick, the inarticulate - seeing and thinking and feeling as he or she does.

Seeing people through God's eyes - the God who values each individual so much that he sent his own Son into the world to die for our sake. And then seeing the world through the eyes of our suffering brothers and sisters in the human family.

This can be very challenging, very demanding. It involves trying to imagine and understand what it means to be a single parent, or a widow, or unemployed with family responsibilities and little prospect of work, or leaving school with little hope for future, or what it's like to be an addict, or a refugee.

This involves using God's gift of imagination and trying to understand how it feels to live in someone else's world, what it's like to sit there surrounded by hungry dying people, and with a gnawing, empty sensation in your own stomach, or imagining how it feels to watch others die and wondering when it will be my turn.

Blessed are the merciful, for they will be shown mercy

There is nothing airy-fairy here. This has nothing to do with light prison sentences or excusing wrongdoers at the expense of those wronged. Jesus is calling for practical action, calling for us to face a demanding challenge, calling us to ask ourselves some hard questions.

Am I merciful towards the needy? Am I compassionate towards the oppressed? What's my attitude towards those who have backslidden? Am I at all concerned about those who have, as it were, fallen off the ladder and who are finding it very hard to climb back on again? What's my attitude towards those who lack many of my privileges? Or am I callous and impatient, hard-hearted and indifferent?

There was a time when, as a Baptist minister, I would take the Baptist Times each week. In addition to this I would also take the Church Times just to make sure I was aware of what was happening beyond my own denomination. There was an editorial in the Church Times on one occasion – I saved it because I believe it makes an important point in terms of being merciful. Let me close by quoting this editorial:

Claims on the mind of the merciful continue without end. No part of the world is immune from misfortune. Sometimes the disaster is man-made, sometimes natural, sometimes a compound of the two... As distresses multiply, so do the appeals. Each time, the Christian is asked to respond with more than prayer. Cheerful giving abounds; yet it is still possible to encounter, or to discover in oneself, arguments against giving - arguments rooted in the imperfections of human beings.

'I'd give if I thought it was all going to go to those in need - but it doesn't. So much is spent on administration and publicity'

'I'd give but there's so much corruption in these countries - the aid never gets to those who need it, but it is creamed off by those in power

'Why should we give when the money is spent on developing nuclear arms?'

And so we hear these and other excuses. It is neither reasonable nor right to demand that all aid should flow through clean channels to worthy recipients. To do so is to apply stiffer tests to others than we apply to ourselves. The unworthiness, the need for mercy, is in the end the same on all sides: only the circumstances are different. The Christian answer is to extend to them the same forgiveness as one is oneself in need of.

Jesus said: Blessed are the merciful, for they will be shown mercy

Chapter Six

Blessed are the pure in heart…

(Matthew 5:8)

Blessed are the pure in heart, for they will see God

When Edwina Currie (at that time Secretary of State for Health) both condemned and offended Northerners for their diet of 'chips with everything', and their generally unhealthy eating habits, not only was she missing the point that a healthy diet sometimes comes at a cost, whether financially, or in terms of time needed to prepare food in a household where both adults may need to work simply to survive and pay the bills, but she was reflecting a growing interest in healthy living. This continues to simmer in today's society even though, twenty of so years on, unhealthy eating has not really decreased significantly and obesity, especially among the young, is now described as being a global concern.

Many people's food choices may not have improved very much but there is today more information available, even on food packaging, to overcome ignorance and to allow better choices to be made when doing the weekly shopping.

Some, of course, take the interest in health foods to extremes so that they become obsessed and neurotic but, by and large, a healthy diet, together with regular exercise, is to be encouraged. Unfortunately since middle-age arrived and I have journeyed on into retirement, my diet and exercise have literally gone 'pear-shaped'. (The reader would understand if he or she could see my profile!)

Today our health professionals encourage fitness, adequate exercise, plenty of fibre in our diet, not too much salt or sugar, and an awareness of our cholesterol levels, all aimed at reducing disease, and in particular, heart disease. The aim is to keep our arteries clear and unrestricted, and to keep poisons and impurities out of our bloodstream.

The first half of sixth Beatitude could well be an appropriate slogan, therefore, for a campaign by the Department of Health - **Blessed are the pure in heart.** And I am sure that Jesus would agree. Surely he would encourage healthy living, a proper diet, and a respect for our bodies. But all this is not really what Jesus had in mind in this Beatitude.

As is the case with the English language, the Greeks only had one word for 'heart', and this one word was used both physically and figuratively.

Jesus is using 'heart' figuratively here, with the heart being our control centre, the centre of our thoughts and desires and motivation. And Jesus says **Blessed are the pure in heart.**

We ought first of all to underline the phrase 'in heart'. Jesus is not concerned here with appearances, externals, things we can see. This is not about outward purity but inward purity. Indeed, this is always Jesus' primary concern. Later in Matthew 5:21-24 we read: **"You have heard that it was said to the people long ago, 'You shall not murder, and anyone who murders will be subject to judgment.' But I tell you that anyone who is angry with a brother or sister will be subject to judgment. Again, anyone who says to a brother or sister, 'Raca,' is answerable to the court. And anyone who says, 'You fool!' will be in danger of the fire of hell. "Therefore, if you are offering your gift at the altar and there remember that your brother or sister has something against you, leave your gift there in front of the altar. First go and be reconciled to them; then come and offer your gift.**

And then in verses 27-28, Jesus says: **"You have heard that it was said, 'You shall not commit adultery.' But**

I tell you that anyone who looks at a woman lustfully has already committed adultery with her in his heart.

Jesus looks deeply. He sees beneath the veneer, the façade, and he looks right inside at the condition of the heart.

Jesus could have said **Blessed are the pure** and left it at that, but if he had said this then he would easily have been misunderstood, especially by his fellow Jews. After all, they knew all about outward purification. They had their elaborate rules for worship. They had their prescribed and precise rituals aimed at preparing them for worship. All the symbolic washing, and cleansing and purification rites. Indeed, the Pharisees and Scribes made a career out of purity and keeping clean. They religiously kept the Law, carefully setting aside their tithes, keeping everything pure and clean. But Jesus saw through the outward appearances and the hypocrisy, as seen very clearly in Matthew 23:23-28 –

"Woe to you, teachers of the law and Pharisees, you hypocrites! You give a tenth of your spices—mint, dill and cumin. But you have neglected the more important matters of the law—justice, mercy and faithfulness. You should have practiced the latter, without neglecting the former. You blind guides! You strain out a gnat but swallow a camel. Woe to you, teachers of the law and Pharisees, you hypocrites! You clean the outside of the cup and dish, but inside they are full of greed and self-indulgence. Blind Pharisee! First clean the inside of the cup and dish, and then the outside also will be clean. Woe to you, teachers of the law and Pharisees, you hypocrites! You are like whitewashed tombs, which look beautiful on the outside but on the inside are full of the bones of the dead and everything unclean. In the same way, on the outside you appear to people as righteous but on the inside you are full of hypocrisy and wickedness."

Blessed are the pure in heart. What does this mean? The Greek word translated 'pure' means 'unmixed, unadulterated, undiluted'. A pure heart is one that does not contain conflicting motives and demands. A pure heart does not pursue a course of action as a means to end. A pure heart is honest not because 'honesty is the best policy' but because honesty is right and proper and good. A pure heart does not perform good works to win favour with God or man, but because it is the will of God that we should be thoughtful and kind and loving. A pure heart is a single-minded heart.

In Luke chapter nine we read of a man whom Jesus called to follow him. What a privilege, to be called to be a disciple of Jesus. Jesus could obviously see some potential in this man, which is why he called him to be one of his followers. But the man was not single-minded. 'Lord, first let me go and bury my father.' he said. Can you see a contradiction there? If Jesus really was his 'Lord', then the man would have obeyed straightaway. 'Lord, first let me go and bury my father'. Not that father had died yet, because if he had, he would have been buried within hour or so of death! That was the custom at that time. Jesus not calling this man out of a funeral procession! What the man was really saying was 'I'd love to follow you, but first let me stay with my father until he's dead, and then I'll come with you.' He was not single-minded.

'Pure in heart' then means a heart that is uncluttered by all kinds of conflicting demands and ulterior motives. This is not new teaching Jesus is offering here though. He is simply reminding people of God's message in the Old Testament, For example, in 1 Samuel 16:7 we read **Man looks at the outward appearance, but the Lord looks at the heart.** Psalm 24:3f **Who may ascend the hill of the Lord? - who may stand in his holy place? He who has clean hands and a pure heart.** Isaiah spoke God's message condemning empty worship. Hosea spoke out against insincere worship and empty words. Joel, Amos and the rest of the prophets underlined the message.

Blessed are the pure in heart... Blessed are those whose motives are pure, clean, unmixed. Blessed are those whose sole (or 'soul'! spell it how you like!) - whose sole aim is to serve God above all else. Blessed are those who are ready 'to labour and to ask for no reward, save that of knowing that we do Thy will'.

And Jesus goes on to say that the blessing is this... **they will see God.** First of all this means that the pure in heart will see God *here and now.* Not, of course, with the naked eye. Not by means of light signals gathered on the retina of the eye and interpreted by our brain cells. Not 'see' in the normal physical sense of seeing. This is not what Jesus means.

The kind of sight Jesus has in mind is that of recognising God who is present and active in the world and in people and all around us. Creation itself is a mirror reflecting thehand of God. We can 'see', perceive God in the world of nature, but so many people are blind.

There are many situations and places where we can discern God's presence. We can be sure, for example, that God will be present in places where people are suffering, and his presence becomes visible through those who care for and reach out to suffering people. We can discern God at times calling us in particular ways, challenging us to action. God is, of course, always present at all times and in all places, but we don't always perceive his presence or his activity.

Jesus saw his heavenly Father everywhere he went, but he was saddened by the blindness of so many of his disciples. And here in this Beatitude he diagnoses the cause of this blindness. It is caused by a heart condition.

In his famous book Lewis Carroll causes Alice, of Wonderland fame, to say: 'A cat may look at a king.' John Ruskin wisely adds: 'Yes, but can a cat see a king?'

We can look, but do we see? We can admire the world around us, but do we see the God who created the world and who is present in his world? We can look in on all kinds of situations and see terrible human tragedy and suffering, but can we see, perceive God in those places? Can we perceive signs of his greatness, majesty, mercy, love, holiness? It all depends on the condition of the heart.

Jesus says the pure in heart are blessed here and now for they are able to see God, to perceive the hand of God, to discern his presence in our everyday world. But there will also come a day when everyone will see God. Sooner or later we all have to stand before almighty God and give an account of our lives and listen to what he thinks of us. And some, given the choice, would rather not see God, thank you very much! Jesus himself said that some would prefer to be buried alive than face God (Luke 23:30). It is God's desire and purpose that all shall see him face to face and it is God's will that all should anticipate this day with eagerness and excitement, and with peace and joy and assurance in hearts, because we believe that God will look at us and see, not our sinfulness and guilt but the purity and holiness of his Son, the crucified Christ who died in our place.

Everyone will see God one day, but not all will remain in his presence. The blessing of this Beatitude is that the pure in heart will see God face-to-face and remain in God's glorious presence for ever. This promise is for the pure in heart, not the curious, not the proud and arrogant who say 'Show me and then I'll believe!', not the intellectual (at least not by virtue of their intellect), not the wealthy . It is for those who have clean hands and a pure heart, those who are single-minded, who have pure motives, whose intentions are genuine, who long wholeheartedly to see God – such will be blessed and will see God indeed.

What a privilege! The Jews were a privileged people, a chosen race, called out from among all the peoples of the earth. They were given clear instructions on how to approach God in worship, and how to purify themselves, how to draw near to God and live in fellowship with him. They were indeed a privileged people. But as believers and followers of Jesus we are called to even higher privilege – to see God in the here and now, and in the future to see him face to face, without fear. This is our 'hope in glory', and what a family gathering that will be! A gathering of the redeemed, in the presence of God the Father, and of Christ our elder brother.

I don't know what your idea of heaven is, but this is the Biblical picture - eternal fellowship with God, face to face.

As for now, we can only guess, speculate as to just what that will be like. The apostle Paul says that now 'we see through a glass darkly, we see just a just dim reflection in mirror, but then we shall see clearly.' This is the whole essence of the Christian hope - to see and to know, to love and be loved by the Father and the Son in the company of God's vast family.

Now this is a prospect that should really excite us, but it should also frustrate.

Blessed are the pure in heart, for they will see God.
You see, these words of Jesus should at least make us stop and think. Blessed is the person whose motives are always pure, sincere, unmixed, unadulterated, undiluted by selfish concerns? If we are honest, we have to confess that very rarely do we have unmixed motives. Whatever good we do, whatever sacrificial act we perform, whatever job well done, whatever sermon well-preached, whatever… we should ask the question 'Why? What was my motive?' And if we are honest somewhere in our answer we may detect a touch of self-satisfaction, pride, pleasure in being praised and thanked.

This Beatitude invites us to ask some awkward questions of ourselves. 'What do I think of when my mind slips into neutral?' 'What do I want more than anything else?' 'Where do my **real** affections lie?' 'Where does God fit into my plans and ambitions?' 'When I carry out some form of service, some act of kindness, what do I expect to gain, receive, get out of it?'

Very rarely is the honest answer likely to be 'To see God, to draw nearer to him, to know him better, to catch a glimpse of his glory.'

So then, how can we be this pure? The answer is 'With great difficulty!' In fact, it is impossible! There is not a day passes but we have cause to confess our sins and failures. We fall short of the glory of God, God's standards, and our own standards too. Isaiah puts it even more vividly – **All our righteous acts are like filthy rags!** So, how can be cleansed completely, purified? The answer is 'By the blood of the Lamb who takes away the sin of the world.' By the death of Christ. And only through faith in Christ can we be made pure and fit to see God.

And when we have been cleansed, purged, renewed, how do we remain pure?

Jesus gave two great commandments. When the Hebrew slaves were set free from Egypt, they were given ten commandments to show them how to live as God's people. Jesus gave two commandments, and if we want to remain pure, it is essential that we keep the two in the right order.

The second commandment is **Love your neighbour as yourself** but the all-important first commandment is **Love the Lord your God with all your heart, soul and mind**.

Here's how to purify our motives when we serve our neighbour, or engage in acts of mercy, or when we undertake some form of service in the church or the community. First and foremost we must love God will all our heart, soul and mind, with our whole being and the whole of life. This is the foundation of everything else.

Love the Lord your God with all heart, soul, mind

Chapter Seven

Blessed are the peacemakers...

(Matthew 5: 9)

Blessed are the peacemakers, for they will be called sons of God

Several years ago Bernard Green, a former General Secretary of the Baptist Union, wrote an article entitled: 'Towards a Theology and Practice of Peace-making', and among other things, Bernard Green said this: 'Our conduct depends on the kind of God we believe in...' He went on to say this: 'Although the Old Testament contains many passages depicting God as using military power to achieve his purposes, the steadily unfolding understanding of the nature of God, fully expressed in the life and death of Christ, clearly reveals a *God of peace*.'

'Our conduct depends on the kind of God we believe in...' In other words, whether we are peace-*makers* or peace-*breakers* depends on our personal understanding and experience of God. Indeed, in the light of this seventh Beatitude, we can put it another way and say that whether we are peace-*makers* or peace-*breakers* depends on whose children we are. Is our God and Father a mighty, victorious warrior, destroying all who stand in his way? Or is he better described as 'the God and Father of our Lord Jesus Christ?'

The apostle Paul spent the earlier part of his life not only under a different name - Saul - but he also spent it believing, as a Jew, that his nation had been chosen by God, and therefore this must mean that the Jewish nation was intended to be the supreme nation, ruling over everyone else. The problem was that their understanding of the nature and character of God was defective, incomplete, with the result that their understanding of their purpose as a nation was also defective and incomplete.

Paul had been brought up in this belief, and yet in 2 Corinthians 5 he writes this: **God reconciled us to himself through Christ and gave us the ministry of reconciliation.** Or as the Good News Bible puts it, **Christ changed us from enemies into his friends and gave us the task of making others his friends also.**

Paul, that most enthusiastic and zealous of Jews, says that God's children are to be peacemakers. Why did Paul say this? Because on the Road to Damascus, where he was heading with the intention of stamping out all the followers of Jesus, Christ himself came and revealed the truth about God to Paul. Paul's conduct was changed because Paul's understanding of God was changed. He became a new man because he was given a new understanding of the character of God. Paul became a peace-*maker* instead of a peace-*breaker* because he met the Prince of Peace and now believed in the God of peace.

Let's just remind selves of meaning of this word 'peace'. Biblically, 'peace' is not just the absence of conflict. The Hebrew word is 'Shalom'. When a Jew greets a fellow Jew with the word 'Shalom', he is expressing far more than the hope of no war, conflict, violence. 'Shalom' means 'wholeness', total wellbeing, complete harmony at every level of existence, health of body, mind and spirit. This is the meaning of 'peace', and in this seventh Beatitude, Jesus is commending and blessing peacemakers, those who create and promote and nurture this peace, this wholeness.

Notice that Jesus says 'peace*makers*', not just peace-*lover*. This is not just about being *peaceful,* or about having a deep longing for peace. And neither did Jesus say Blessed are the peace-*keepers*. Peacekeeping is quite a different matter.

In 1873, Samuel Colt created a new type of pistol. It had a simple design, and used a new type of cartridge so that anyone could learn to use this weapon. This pistol was easy to load and a new improved sight made it simple to aim and fire. It was said that God made every man different but that Samuel Colt made them equal - the idea being that a larger, stronger man could no longer overpower a smaller, weaker man. What had previously been a matter of strength was now a matter of speed and accuracy. The name given to this new type of pistol was *'The Peacekeeper.'*

In November 1982, President Ronald Reagan named the new mobile M-X missile *'The Peacekeeper.'* The idea was that this missile, with its greater mobility and its modern guidance systems, would be a powerful deterrent to foreign aggression.

It is interesting, isn't it, that in these two examples the word 'peacekeeper' is associated with weapons? In fact, if you make an internet search with the word 'peacekeeper,' many of the references are to weapons, soldiers, wars, although, to be fair, I did find another use of the word. America's biggest plumbing manufacturer is marketing a product that could save countless marriages. It's called the 'Peacekeeper' and it is a toilet that won't flush unless the seat is down! There is also a boot called a Peacemaker. It is made in Yorkshire and is supplied to armed forces and the police and security firms. But by and large, the impression is that if are going to set about keeping the peace, you are going to need weapons.

The problem is that we send peacekeeping forces to keep the peace where there is no real peace to be kept.

'Keeping the peace' then is about avoiding trouble, making sure there is no conflict, no fighting and it amounts to no more than keeping the hatred and aggression under wraps.

Peace-*making* is more positive and is to do with actively

promoting wholeness, harmony, seeking a person's highest good, working for the very best outcome for a person or a group of people, and it includes social concern, political awareness and action, a ministry of reconciliation, and evangelism. Peace-*making* is about dealing with the root causes of conflict and disharmony.

But before we rush off and start getting involved in social action and political campaigning and other aspects of mission, we need to understand one or two basic requirements if we are going to be peacemakers.

First of all we need to have **peace with God**, and we cannot have peace with God other than through the Lord Jesus Christ, the greatest peace-maker ever, the Prince of Peace. It is in Jesus Christ and him alone that we have peace. Ephesians 2: 13: **But now in Christ Jesus you who once were far away have been brought near through the blood of Christ. For he himself is our peace.** In 1 Corinthians 1, Paul refers to God making **'peace through Christ's blood shed on the cross'**. There is no other way - only in Christ can we find real peace with God.

Secondly, a peace-maker needs not only to be at peace with God but also at peace with him or herself. Much of the conflict between people is rooted in inner strife. We are often not at peace within ourselves. We feel insecure, dissatisfied, inadequate, uncomfortable and we have an internal conflict. And often we off-load our insecurity and our feelings of guilt and failure, dissatisfaction and inadequacy on to others. Sometimes we do this through gossip and destructive criticism, sometimes by demanding of others the perfection we can't seem to find in ourselves/

Peace with God should create peace with ourselves, for isn't the gospel message saying that we are special to God? Isn't it saying that in spite of our failures, our sins, God still loves us. He is our loving heavenly Father and we are his precious, dearly loved children. Doesn't the gospel say that our security and therefore our peace are to be found in him and in a relationship with our Father?

Thirdly, peace-making begins with peace with God which brings peace with ourselves, but then has to find positive expression in our relationships with other people.

Robert Louis Stevenson tells a true story of two sisters who lived together in Edinburgh, in a large two-bedded room, each sister having her own furniture. One day the sisters quarrelled over whose turn it was to wind the clock. One sister said something sharp and unkind that hurt the other sister, who responded with something even more hurtful. And so it went on. The result? For 50 years - FIFTY years! – they never spoke. They drew a chalk line on the floor and divided the room into two halves, each having half the fire and half the door - presumably it was a double door. For fifty years each sister lived on her own side of the line. They grew old and frail in the sight of each other but neither ever crossed the line to help her sister. If only one of them had been a peace-*maker,* all that stupidity would have ended. And to think, it all began over something quite trivial.

We need to be peace-makers in our families to prevent that sort of thing happening.

And we need to be peace-makers in our church fellowships! Isn't it sad when God's people quarrel? Isn't it sad the way some people treat their brothers and sisters in Christ? Isn't it sad that some people seem to delight in divisions, and go out of their way to make mischief and cause conflict between other people. Promoting division and disharmony, bitterness and unhappiness and strife in a Christian fellowship is sinful, and it grieves our heavenly Father.

'But,' we may say. 'some people are just so touchy, so easily upset. How can we live in peace and harmony when some people are so oversensitive?'

A boy was once sent to the head teacher to explain why he had been involved in a fight in the playground. The boy made the excuse that the other boy had been making a fuss over nothing. 'He's always like that; so touchy! He reacts at the least little thing.' 'In that case' said the head teacher, 'why did you throw your sparks so close to his gunpowder?'

Part of the task of peace-making is taking into consideration the other person's weaknesses.

Apparently there's a popular picnic spot near some mountains in North America. The mountains are covered with gorse, which becomes very dry in the summer. Near this picnic spot is a notice which says: 'Don't let fires start. They are hot, and often run faster than you can'

Now that sounds like good advice for any would-be peace-maker! 'Don't let fires start. They are hot, and often run faster than you can'

We need peace-makers in our churches, and here's what this means in practice. I came across this simple suggestion a while ago, and it really does sound simple, but I believe this would revolutionise our lives and the life of Christ's church if we put it into practice. Here's this simple suggestion:- If you are going to make a comment about someone (whether it's a person you know personally or even some celebrity in news) ask yourself this question: Will this comment build that person's reputation or destroy it?

Our response to this question, our inclination to gossip or to refrain from gossiping, our indulgence in character assassination or character promotion, will show us whether we are peace *makers* or peace *breakers.*

We need peacemakers in our homes and families, in our churches, in our local communities and in the wider world. Remember, peace-making means creating, nurturing and promoting a person's, or a group of people's, well-being, shalom, wholeness.

Quoting Bernard Green again: 'Christian peace-making today must include taking away people's sense of hopelessness and helplessness, that feeling that the problems are too big and they can do nothing.'

This means expressing in practical ways God's love which we ourselves have first experienced in Christ. Opportunities for this present themselves on a daily basis, whether it's in the supermarket, or the post office queue, in our driving habits, in welcoming strangers (regardless of colour of skin, or religion, or culture) – opportunities for peace-making present themselves on a daily basis.

And peace-making must always include promoting peace and wholeness in the wider world where many people are desperately poor, and hungry. There are, of course, many channels for doing this, by giving our money, or even ourselves.

When we begin to see the range of opportunities for peace-making, then we also begin to realise this is another of those things limited only by our imaginations.

Jesus says: **Blessed are the peacemakers, for they will be called sons of God.**

But he doesn't say it will always be easy. Indeed peace-making can sometimes be hard and costly. After all, what happened to the Prince of Peacemakers? He ended up on a cross. Other peacemakers have been assassinated or imprisoned and tortured, or ostracised, separated from family and from the community.

Peace-making won't always be easy, but Jesus says peace makers will be blessed. How? He says **'they will be called 'Sons of God'**. This is an expression with a special meaning. Let me try and explain.

The New Testament was, of course, originally written in Greek. Jesus spoke in Aramaic, so the Greek is a translation of the Aramaic. The Aramaic language is not a very rich language. Some languages, such as English, have a rich vocabulary, meaning that they have a word for everything and several words for some things, often representing different shades of meaning. In the case of English, the richness of our language reflects the fact that we have been invaded on a number of occasions and absorbed the language of our invaders.

The Aramaic language does not have a very rich vocabulary. For example, it does not have a word meaning 'peaceful'. In Aramaic, if you wanted to say someone was peaceful, you would have to say he was a 'son of peace'. If they were compassionate then that person would be a 'son of compassion', if stormy, or boisterous, then he would be a 'son of thunder'. 'Son of...' means 'like, resembling, having the nature of...'

In Daniel 7 we come across the Aramaic[1] expression 'son of man' - **'there before me was one like a son of man, coming with the clouds of heaven'** This simply means 'someone resembling a human being'. If someone is called a 'son of the Devil', it means he is evil, showing the character of Satan.

'Blessed are the peacemakers for they will be called sons of God' means that something of God's nature will be seen in them - perhaps just a pale reflection compared with God himself but enough to be reminded of the character of God. The blessing is that God will also look and see something of himself in the peace-maker. He will look and see a reflection of his own nature, and he will own us, recognise us as his children because he himself is the God of peace.

---

[1] Much of the Book of Daniel was originally written in Aramaic.

So the question is, what you going to be? A peace-*maker* or a peace-*breaker*? A peace-*maker* who delights in promoting unity and harmony and wholeness, or a peace-*breaker* who takes pleasure in division and conflict and unhappiness?

Are you going to be a peace-*maker,* like Monica the mother of St Augustine who described his mother in this way: 'She showed herself such a peacemaker between factious and quarrelsome people that, though she listened to many bitter words from both sides, she would never repeat to one what another said, unless it were something which might tend to reconcile them.'

Are you going to be like that? Or a peace-*breaker* like John Lilburne of whom Cromwell said: 'John Lilburne is so cantankerous that, if he couldn't find anyone else to quarrel with, John would quarrel with Lilburne and Lilburne would quarrel with John!'

One final comment which reminds us of what's needed if we are to become peacemakers. Phillip Keller wrote a book some years ago called 'A Shepherd Looks at the 23rd Psalm', a book written out of his own experiences working for eight years as a shepherd. In the book Keller goes through the 23rd Psalm, explaining it from the point of view of a shepherd. At one point he explains that there is a pecking order in the sheep, and that sometimes this creates conflict among the sheep. 'Hundreds of times I have watched an old ewe walk up to a younger one which might have been feeding quite happily, or resting quietly in some sheltered spot. The old ewe would arch her neck, tilt her head, dilate her eyes and approach the younger sheep in a menacing way. The body language was saying in unmistakable terms, 'Move over! Out of my way! Give way or else!' And if the other sheep didn't immediately leap to her feet in self-defence, she would be butted unmercifully. Or, if she did rise to accept the challenge, one or two strong bumps would soon send her scurrying for safety. But one point always interested me very much. Whenever I came into view and my presence was noticed, the sheep quickly forgot their foolish rivalries and stopped their fighting.'

The shepherd's presence made all the difference in their behaviour. And the Good Shepherd's presence, living in us, inspires and enables us to be peacemakers, forgetting our foolish rivalries and stopping our fighting.

Blessed are the peacemakers, for they will be called sons of God

Chapter Eight

Blessed are those who are persecuted for righteousness sake...

(Matthew 5:10-12)

On June 11th 2004, more than one hundred leaders of the China Gospel Fellowship were arrested. The arrests took place at Wuhan city, while these church leaders were meeting together. According to a senior house church leader and an eyewitness of the arrests, about 50 police, believed to be from the Public Security Bureau of Wuhan City, raided the church meeting at around 2pm and arrested all of the participants, including one of the senior Fellowship leaders, Mr Xing Jinfu. Mr Xing had been arrested at least three times before for his church activities. In 1996 he was sentenced to three years 're-education through labour' for his 'illegal preaching'.

In the same year, 2004, in Sri Lanka two new laws threatened to put further pressure on Christians who had already suffered dozens of violent attacks during that year. The Buddhist nationalist party. the Jathika Hela Urumaya, was planning to present an anti-conversion bill to Parliament. In addition, Sri Lanka's new Minister of Buddhism announced that he would introduce legislation to ban 'deceitful' spreading of the Christian message.

In Pakistan a Christian accused of blasphemy was savagely attacked in the name of religion, this time allegedly by a policeman. Despite being under police protection, Samuel Masih, was hit around the head with a brick cutter, having been admitted to hospital with tuberculosis. He has since died from serious head injuries. Samuel Masih was accused of throwing waste against the wall of a mosque and was beaten up by a Muslim prayer leader and others in Lahore, and then handed over to the police. He was arrested on August 23, 2003 and held in Lahore Central Jail, where he remained until May 22, 2004, when he was admitted to hospital suffering from tuberculosis. A police guard was provided for his security in the hospital, but on May 24 at 4.30am, a police constable attacked him.

In the same year at least 48 people were hacked to death by armed Muslims in Yelwa, Nigeria, during an early morning prayer service. Armed Muslims invaded the service, ordered the congregation to lie face down and proceeded 'to machete and axe them to death in their house of worship' according to the Christian Association of Nigeria. The victims included women and children. A further upsurge in violence in Nigeria claimed at least 100 lives. During the period between February and May 2004 over 700 people were killed.

This is how it was back in 2004 when I first preached this sermon, but in many ways, the situation hasn't really changed very much.[2] Christians are still being persecuted in these places, along with other countries such as Cuba, Vietnam, Burma, India, Peru, Sudan, Saudi Arabia, Egypt and many more places.

Jesus said: **Blessed are those who are persecuted because of righteousness, for theirs is the Kingdom of heaven.** It is easy to see that these words of Jesus are as relevant today (if not more so) as when they were first spoken, especially when we remember that persecution is not restricted to physical violence, torture, death threats and imprisonment, but includes situations where faithful Christians may find themselves ridiculed or rejected by members of their family, or sneered at by colleagues.

Clearly this eighth and last Beatitude has something to say to us today in the twenty-first century.

Blessed are those who are persecuted because of righteousness... This has been described as 'the blessing no one wants'! It seems to be a blessing we are quite

---

[2] For up-to-date news and regular updates by email, see www.csw.org, the website of Christian Solidarity Worldwide.

happy to do without! But it is also a blessing that will come our way if the first seven beatitudes make any impact on our lives. You see, if we live our lives according to the profile described by Jesus here in these verses, it is safe to say we will experience some degree of persecution.

Live the Jesus way and you had better be ready for a hard time.

Blessed are those who are persecuted because of righteousness... What do we mean by righteousness? Back in chapter four we looked at 'righteousness' in more detail but to put it succinctly, 'righteousness' means quite simply 'right living'. And we could say this righteousness is described for us in the first seven Beatitudes, in the radical way of living demanded by Christ. This eighth Beatitude (along with vv 11, 12) spells out for us the likely reception the world will give us if we live in this way.

If we're 'Poor in Spirit' people will think we're being 'self-righteous.' If we 'Mourn and Repent over sin', they'll be offended because they'll feel we're being 'holier than thou'. Be 'Meek and Humble' and they'll try to push take advantage and test our limits. If we 'Hunger after Righteousness' we'll be labelled a 'narrow-minded, religious fanatic.' Be 'Merciful' and watch them laugh and shake their heads in disbelief - and call us do-gooders. Be 'Pure in Heart' and struggle against the tide in a world dedicated to pleasure at all costs. Strive to be a 'Peacemaker' and be ready for all kinds of ammunition pointed in our direction by those who feed on conflict. And put all these together in one life (which is what we are meant to do), and then stand by for a reaction. It's an explosive mixture and the world will try to dilute it to make such a life less effective, less powerful. Persecution is the weapon of choice against a life dedicated to doing the will of God.

I came across an interesting observation in an old book

some time ago. Referring to this Beatitude, the writer said: 'Every community tends to demand of its members a certain average of conduct. It dislikes anyone who is conspicuously worse or better than the average. If we fall much below the average we are fined or imprisoned. If we rise much above the average, we are persecuted.' In other words society prefers mediocrity! But Jesus is not calling us to an average life of mediocrity. He challenges us to do better than average, whilst at the same time being realistic about the cost of such a way of life. Jesus prepares his followers for the stark reality that following Christ involves carrying a cross.

The plain truth is that the world doesn't like those who appear to be different. Let's face it - **we** don't like people who are a bit odd, eccentric and who don't seem to be playing by the same rules. We can sometimes feel threatened by people who appear to be different. And to non-believers, those of us who live the Jesus way can seem to be odd, eccentric, and operating according to a different set of rules, which we are, or should be!

Blessed are those who are persecuted because of righteousness, says Jesus, for theirs is the kingdom of heaven. And then what does he say? Well, just in case we think he's just generalising and all this does not really apply to us, Jesus goes on to say: **'Blessed are you when people insult you, persecute you and falsely say all kinds of evil against you because of me.'** Jesus makes it personal, and then he says **Rejoice and be glad for great is your reward**

What exactly is the reward, the blessing? **for theirs is the kingdom of heaven.** As with the first Beatitude, this simply means 'they belong to God'. Those who stand the test of opposition because they are determined to remain faithful and obedient show that they are already living in the Kingdom of God, already living under the authority of the King of kings.

Therefore, says Jesus, rejoice and be glad! It may not

always be easy. When a cross is placed on my back I am more likely to wince than smile! But what this means is that, at least, we should stifle any feelings of bitterness or resentment. Don't complain when called upon to carry a cross, don't harbour any desire for revenge. After all, opposition is a sign that we are walking in God's way, following in the steps of Jesus. Persecution is a sign that we are rattling the Devil's cage and opposing his evil plans and exposing his evil lies.

Rejoice and be glad! because you are in good company, says Jesus. **In the same way they persecuted the prophets who were before you.** The Old Testament prophets did not have an easy time. They too sometimes suffered abuse and physical violence. Hosea was called to deliver an unpopular message, calling for repentance, criticising the leaders of the nation and their policies, exposing the idolatry of the people of God in all its many forms. He met with hostility but stood firm.

Isaiah, Jeremiah, Amos were all persecuted for doing what God required, but remained faithful and received their reward.

But what does all this mean for us, living here in 21st century England? Throughout the Beatitudes Jesus has taken the message of society and turned it on its head, and this eighth Beatitude is no exception. Persecution is not regarding as a blessing by the rest of society. The message of society is quite the opposite. Conform! Do you want to be successful? Conform! Do you want a quiet life? Conform! Do you want a peaceful existence? Conform! Don't be the odd one out! It isn't worth it. Conform! Do what everyone else does. Adopt the standards, morality, values of society. Go with the crowd. Stay in line. After all, it won't harm anyone if you add a little extra to your expenses claim, or if you bend the truth a little on your tax return, or if you can manage to get away with some other dishonest practice. It won't hurt anyone. Everyone does it.

Advertisers scream the same message at us - conform!
'Everyone's going to such and such a place',
'Everyone's buying such and such a product'. I always
want to ask: 'If that's true why are you so desperate for
me to buy your product as well? Why are you spending
millions just to get me to buy it?'

They show us luxurious homes, and consumer goods and
the latest cars, and they create the impression everyone's
got it or everyone wants it - conform! That's the message
of society.

But we belong to a non-conformist tradition, and I am
not thinking here of the free church as distinct from the
established church. I am thinking of a non-conformist
tradition going back 2000 years. The Christian Church at
its best has always been non-conformist. Stephen, the
first Christian martyr, was a non-conformist. Each
generation of Christians has been called to be non-
conformists, facing persecution for righteousness' sake –
persecution coming from beyond the church, but sadly
also persecution coming from within the Christian
Church. The history of my own denomination – Baptist –
is one of persecution by other branches of Christianity.
John Wesley suffered from his fellow churchmen. It cost
lives to have the Bible in our own language – Wycliffe,
Tyndale were both true non-conformists. Thomas
Cranmer, whose liturgies were the basis of the Book of
Common Prayer, was burned at stake.

But this is non-conformity not just for the sake of being
different. It is non-conformity for righteousness' sake,
for Jesus' sake, because it is about doing what God
requires.

All of this invites us to consider our own lives. First of
all, is there any sense in which we ourselves might be
persecut**ors**? Is there any sense in which we ourselves
might be making it harder for someone else to remain
faithful and obedient to Christ? We are called to build
one another up, not to pull each other down or tear each

other apart! Is there any sense in which we dislike or resent anyone who is conspicuously better than average, or who is simply different?

Secondly, this Beatitude invites us to consider our own life. If no one ever tries to sneer at us, or makes life difficult because of our faith, why is that? Could it be because we have not really taken the Beatitudes seriously? Could it be that we have not allowed these words of Jesus to have any real impact on our lives? And there is nothing worth attacking as far as the world is concerned?

Blessed are those who are persecuted because of righteousness, for theirs is the kingdom of heaven.

ASPECTS OF LOVE

The Character of a Christian Believer.

A Sermon Series on 'The Fruit of the Spirit'
(Galatians 5: 16-25)

Graeme Stockdale

CONTENTS

Foreword

Chapter One
Introduction

Chapter Two
The fruit of the Spirit is love...

Chapter Three
The fruit of the Spirit is... joy.

Chapter Four
The fruit of the Spirit is... peace

Chapter Five
The fruit of the Spirit is... patience.

Chapter Six
The fruit of the Spirit is... kindness

Chapter Seven
The fruit of the Spirit is... goodness

Chapter Eight
The fruit of the Spirit is... faithfulness

Chapter Nine
The fruit of the Spirit is... gentleness

Chapter Ten
The fruit of the Spirit is... self control

Foreword

In my book 'The Be-Attitudes' I referred to the Beatitudes as being a character profile of a follower of Christ. In some ways the same could be said of the Fruit of the Spirit for here we have a description of the complete disciple, which I believe reflects the character of Christ, and, indeed, of God, as will be seen repeatedly throughout this book. Many, if not all, of these attributes seem to be an impossible dream for most of us and so we will be reminded in this book that this is the work of the Holy Spirit who, among other things, aims to reproduce the character of Christ in the believer. Our task is to consider how best we can facilitate rather than hinder this work, and this book may help us in thinking this through, as we consider these 'aspects of love'.

As in my previous books of sermons, in common with many preachers I have gleaned ideas and sometimes phrases from a wide variety of sources – books, and of course, nowadays, the internet with its wealth of resources. These sermons appeared in the original form over thirty years ago. At the time when the sermons were first written and delivered I did not make a note of sources. I will have used some of William Barclay's teachings regarding the meaning of Greek words, together with various other commentaries, and in revising the sermon, I will have made use of online resources.

I therefore wish to apologise to anyone reading this book who believes that I have made use of their resources without acknowledging the fact. If this is the case, please contact me so that I can at least include an acknowledgement in further updates.

And whilst taking into account my confession, if you are a preacher yourself, and wish to use any of the material in this book, for my part I am happy for you to do this without any acknowledgement, since I believe that these sermons, in truth, belong to God and not to me.

My prayer for you, the reader, is the prayer I have frequently prayed prior to preaching: that the Holy Spirit will inspire you in your reading and thinking so that you may be able to discern God's Word for you in the midst of human language.

Graeme Stockdale
January 2021

Chapter One

Introduction

Galatians 5:16-25

In one of my other books of sermons which I have published – 'Name Above All Names' – I set out a series of sermons on the I AM sayings of Jesus which I suppose could be offered as an answer to the question 'Who is Jesus?' In this current book we move on to another basic question: 'Who am I?'. This is not about me, however. I am not about to write a biography. The question encourages each of us, as believers, to consider what this means in terms of our Christian character. I have already written a book about the Beatitudes, which are also a description of the Christian character; the fruit of the Spirit, described by Paul, supplements the teaching of Jesus on this matter.

In Colossians 1 the apostle Paul tells us who we were: ***once we <u>were</u> strangers, enemies of God*** but he goes on to say that now, through the death of Christ, God has reconciled us, God has changed us from being his enemies to being his friends. But when he's done that, God hasn't finished with us. There is more that he wants to do. Indeed, God's overall aim seems to be for us to become not only friends, but for us to become more and more like Jesus. And the way God sets about this is through the Holy Spirit who, it seems, plants a package of virtues, characteristics deep within us which, if allowed to see the light of day and grow and develop and mature produce what we refer to as 'the fruit of the Spirit'.

We find details of this fruit <u>not</u> listed but described in Galatians 5:22 and 23 in a concise summary of the difference the Holy Spirit wants to make in the life of a believer.

Now, you may have noticed that I just said this fruit is

not listed here in these verses but rather, it is described. Why do I say that? The point I am making is this. In v 22 we do not read ***the fruits of the Spirit <u>are</u> love, joy, peace etc.*** That would be a list, but what it actually says is ***the fruit*** (singular) ***of the Spirit <u>IS</u> love, joy, peace etc***

I believe that this distinction is important and not just playing with words. There are various gifts of the Spirit, but not everyone has the same gifts, and no one has all the gifts. But the 'fruit of the Spirit' describes the qualities which we should expect to find in every believer. It isn't a matter of picking and choosing between, say love on the one hand and kindness, or joy, or peace or patience. Every one of these qualities is meant to be seen in every believer.

Notice also that we are talking about the fruit of the Spirit who is, of course, God himself. These nine words are descriptive of God's character. They do not offer a complete description, but here are words we can use when speaking about God. love, joy, peace, patience, kindness, goodness, faithfulness, gentleness and self-control. And where do we see God's character perfectly displayed? In his Son Jesus Christ in whom we see the family likeness. Because every believer is a child of God, the Holy Spirit works to reproduce the family likeness in us.

The fruit of the Spirit is, of course, very different from the works of the flesh, the acts or character produced by our sinful nature, as Paul describes in earlier verses in Galatians 5. Works of the flesh are the products of human action, but this fruit first and foremost is the work of the Spirit of God.

This fruit is not just a list of natural possibilities you and I can achieve with a little effort (or even a great deal of effort). This is the fruit of the Spirit, the supernatural result of lives yielded to God, the fruit of a renewed nature.

The growth and development of this fruit involves both an emptying and a filling. In his book about the Holy Spirit, Billy Graham, says that the Holy Spirit works like a gate. He points out that a gate can be used for two purposes. It can open to let people in or out, and it can be closed to keep people in or out. Billy Graham says that spiritually our lives are like this. Inside we have all kinds of things that are wrong and displeasing to God, and the gate needs to be opened to let these out, and to allow the Holy Spirit to come in and take control. But, he says, we don't even have the power to open the gate. Only the Holy Spirit can do this. And when he does, he not only comes in but he helps us to get rid of the unholy things in our lives. He controls the gate, and allows the heart to be purged of wickedness; he allows new, wholesome attitudes to gain access, new ways of thinking, a new devotion to God, a new love. And the Holy Spirit strengthens the gate with bars to keep out evil. This fruit, then, is not the result of any effort on our part. It really is the fruit of the Spirit.

Having said this, however, is there anything we can do to help this fruit to grow in our lives? A seed planted in a garden grows of its own accord. There is nothing we can do to make it grow – nothing, that is, except provide the right conditions. The question then is *what conditions encourage fruitfulness*?

Let me suggest two for starters. There may be others, but here are two things we can do to create the right conditions for this fruit to grow.

First of all, **spend more time with Jesus**, through reading the Bible and by talking to him in prayer, doing whatever we can to get to know him better. And secondly, **obey Christ's commands and teachings**. This fruit will not grow properly if we don't follow the instructions.

There is much more that could be said by way of introduction but it is time to move on and look at the first characteristic of this fruit.

Chapter Two

The fruit of the Spirit is love...

There are all kinds of churches - large ones, small ones, evangelical or liberal (or 'middle of the road', whatever that means. I tend to think that the middle of the road is a dangerous place to be!), charismatic or non-charismatic, traditional, contemporary, high, low, strong, weak, inward looking, outward looking, warm, welcoming churches, cold, self-obsessed churches, growing, declining, dynamic, static - all kinds of churches. But when it all boils down, what really matters is this: whether a church is a ***loving*** church or an ***unloving*** church.

No matter what other category we might want to put a church into, what really matters is whether it is a ***loving*** church or an ***unloving*** church, because love is a key word in the Christian faith, it is the heart of the gospel, it is the very essence of God's purpose in creating such an institution as the Church in the first place.

The problem for us is that the word 'love' is one of those English words that has become so devalued that, if we are not careful, our understanding of the word will, at best, be inadequate, and at worst mistaken.

Most of us, I'm sure, will be aware that in Greek there are various words for different kinds of love, but let me remind you for the sake of any who may not know them or who have forgotten them.

One word is the one used for love between a man and a woman (or the various permutations of relationships these days, as, no doubt, in the Greek world). Another word describes love within a family or between friends. And another refers to the love between a parent and child. And then there's the word 'agape', a word used 115 times in the New Testament.

What does 'agape' mean? According to William Barclay, 'agape' means *unconquerable benevolence.* I quite like that definition. Agape also means *persistent love, unconditional love, love that perseveres even in the face of rejection, love that is never defeated.* How does William Barclay arrive at his definition? Well, if we want to know what a Greek word means, there are two things we can do. (a) We can look at the way the Greeks used the word, which doesn't really help us very much because the word was hardly ever used in everyday Greek. (b) We can look at the way the word is used in the New Testament.

Where better to look than Paul's well known 'hymn to love' in 1 Corinthians 13. For example, verse 4 ***love is patient, love is kind, it does not envy, does not boast, is not proud, is not rude, is not self-seeking, is not easily angered, keeps no record of wrongs. Love does not delight in evil but rejoices with the truth. It always protects, always trusts, always hopes, always perseveres. Love never fails***

From this passage alone we can see that 'agape' is a many-splendored thing. What does agape mean? It's here in these verses in 1 Corinthians 13, and Barclay sums it all up in his phrase *'unconquerable benevolence'*

But I wonder if you have ever tried this – take this passage in 1 Corinthians 13:4-8 and instead of the word 'love', try substituting the word 'God'. ***<u>God</u> is patient, <u>God</u> is kind, <u>God</u> does not envy, does not boast, is not proud, is not rude, is not self-seeking, is not easily angered, keeps no record of wrongs. <u>God</u> does not delight in evil but rejoices with the truth. <u>God</u> always protects, always trusts, always hopes, always perseveres. <u>God</u> never fails.***

Whatever else we may say about love, the kind described and referred to, and even commanded, in the New Testament, we can also say about God. This is what the Scriptures mean when we read 'God is love'. We mean all that Paul says in 1 Corinthians 13:4-8. It is a kind of equation - God = love.

Now, when we repent of our sins, and accept Jesus Christ as Lord and Saviour, what happens? The Bible promises that the Holy Spirit is given to us. The Holy Spirit is the Spirit of God, sometimes called the Spirit of Christ, God's living presence deep within us, and he is bound to make a difference! He is bound to bring about some changes in us. It's his main aim, and the fruit of the Spirit is a description of this change that the Holy Spirit works in the hearts and lives of the believer.

The love we are talking about when we say ***the fruit of the Spirit is love...*** is God's love. What other kind of love would we expect the Holy Spirit to give us? If the Spirit of God is living in us, and 'God is love', then the love that the Spirit reproduces in us must be the same love described in 1 Corinthians 13.

This means that when we say ***The fruit of the Spirit is love...*** it means we become ***patient, and kind. We do not envy, do not boast, are not proud, are not rude, are not self-seeking, are not easily angered, keep no record of wrongs.***
We do not delight in evil but rejoice with the truth. We always protect, always trust, always hope, always persevere. (We never fail)

In fact, this is something else worth trying. Instead of saying 'love is patient, love is kind etc,' instead of replacing 'love' by 'God', try putting your own name in there and you'll see a description of the person God through the Holy Spirit is working towards for you.

The Holy Spirit is working to make us like Christ. The Holy Spirit is seeking to promote holiness, true holiness in your life and in mine. Holiness is a word we tend to shy away from, partly because we associate it with the expression 'holier than thou'. Do you know what holiness is? One way of understanding the meaning of 'holiness' is that is means to be Christlike, and the Holy Spirit is seeking to make you and me more like Christ. And it begins with love.

The Holy Spirit fills us with God's love, and then works to create an answering love of the same quality in our lives. So when say ***The fruit of the Spirit is love...*** we are talking about love for God in response to his love for us, and love for one another (as brothers and sisters in Christ), and love for all people, remembering that Christ came into this world as an expression of God's love.

This love here in Galatians 5:22 finds its origin in love of God, which means that God's love is the standard by which we measure our love, and God's love defines the boundaries of our loving. What are those boundaries? Well, can **you** find any limits to God's love for you? The answer is No! there are none! This means that we, in turn, have no business setting limits to our love. And this means that no matter what someone does to us (or to our loved ones), no matter what pain they may cause, no matter what distress, we must never seek anything but their highest good.

This means that we must not let their aggression, their unkindness, their jealousy, envy, malice and so forth conquer and overcome the love which the Holy Spirit creates in us, and that means that such 'love', such 'unconquerable benevolence' concerns the mind and will as much as, if not more than, the heart and feelings. Godly love demands a deliberate effort on our part which we can only make with God's help and strength and support. As someone has put it: *seeking nothing but the best even for those who seek nothing but the worst for us!* or as a child at school once wrote... *You must love your neighbour even if you hate him!* That child, perhaps without knowing it, had caught something of the true meaning of love.

Billy Graham says '*There should be no more distinctive mark of the Christian than love'* and Billy Graham always supports what he says with Scripture... John 13:35 ***By this all men will know that you are my disciples, if you love one another,*** and 1 John 3:14 ***We know that we have passed from death to life (i.e. are Christians) if we love our brothers***

This is because love is a sign that we are allowing the Holy Spirit the freedom to work and act and change our lives into the likeness of Christ.

But is this always the case? Is this distinctive mark always there to identify the Christian? I am not ashamed to say that I would consider myself to be towards the evangelical end of the Christian spectrum. Put simply, this means that the Bible, the Word of God is very important to me. But I am embarrassed by those at the narrow end of evangelicalism where everything seems to be so dark and sombre, monochrome and austere, and where sound doctrine is maintained at all costs. I believe we need to guard the truth. I believe that, not only has the Christian Church suffered and become weak and often ineffective because we have compromised truth, but also our nation is so much the poorer as a consequence. But what saddens me is that those who guard the truth can so often be lacking in love. Those who uphold the doctrine of grace seem so lacking in grace in their human relationships.

This saddens me because when this happens, our witness is compromised and all we are trying to do is wasted; this distinctive New Testament mark of the Christian is not in great evidence. No matter how sound our doctrine, or how moving our testimony may be, without love it means nothing.

Now, of course, it's easy to point the finger at others but the index finger has a habit of curling round and pointing at ourselves. You see, we can easily fall into a trap and our stated opinions of others can so easily stray from the requirements of love. We can point at 'their' lack of love (whoever 'they' may be) and we can do so in an unloving way, and the danger is always there for all of us. Katherine Whitehorn sums it up... ***The story of God's love lost something in the telling when put across by the Spanish Inquisition.*** History is full of similar examples that embarrass and shame us, but it may be that the story of God's love also loses something in the telling when put across by you and me, because we are not allowing the Holy Spirit sufficient freedom to produce his fruit in our lives. The result is the difference between a loving church and an unloving church, a Godly church and an ungodly church.

How then do we measure up? Has the Holy Spirit been able to produce this fruit in our lives - love for the unlovable, love without limits? Or do you share my feeling of failure and inadequacy and shame that I have not allowed the Holy Spirit sufficient freedom to develop this fruit in my life?

The fruit of the Spirit is love... Someone once wrote that the point Paul is making here is this: *if people bite into you* (not literally, I hasten to add!) - *if people bite into you, what do they taste?* And the answer should, of course, be **love!**

Chapter Three

The fruit of the Spirit is… joy.

In a world where there are famines, wars, conflict, personal tragedy and suffering, and a widespread disregard for the sanctity of human life, how on earth can we be joyful? And when we then go on to consider the seriousness of sin, and God's view of sin, and the fact that we are all sinners for whom Christ died, and when we point to the cross of Christ and reflect on the agony and pain and suffering caused by our sins, and furthermore, when we recall that, among other things, Jesus has been described as a 'man of sorrows and acquainted with grief', again, how on earth can we be joyful?

No wonder that for some believers, Christianity is a very serious business. After all, God is a holy, mighty and majestic, awesome, God, and the only appropriate response is one of reverence, which for many is expressed, it seems, in terms of doom and gloom, stern faces, an austere, negative and humourless existence. And yet, the Scriptures speak of all these things, but at the same time exhort us to rejoice! The Scriptures do indeed tell us that Christ is the 'man of sorrows' spoken of by the prophet Isaiah, but that he was also full of the joy of the Holy Spirit. The Scriptures tell us that our lives as Christians should be characterised not only by love but also by joy, a joy that does not ignore or trivialise the reality of the world in which we live, but at the same time, a joy that is not overwhelmed by the immensity and seriousness of it all.

Joy is one of the qualities the Holy Spirit is endeavouring to grow and develop in all believers in order to make us more and more like Christ, but we need first of all to ask the question: **What is joy?**

Let's try some dictionary definitions:

- *Joy is the emotion evoked by well-being, success, or good fortune or by the prospect of possessing what one desires.*
- *Joy is an intense and especially ecstatic or exultant happiness.*
- *Joy is the emotion of great happiness.*
- *Joy is the passion or emotion excited by the acquisition or expectation of good; pleasurable feelings or emotions caused by success, good fortune, and the like, or by a rational prospect of possessing what we love or desire; gladness; exhilaration of spirits; delight*

One of the adverts on TV some time ago was a Cadbury's advert with a 'gorilla' (actually someone dressed in a very lifelike costume) seated at a set of drums, seemingly entranced by either the music or something else. But then, suddenly, he bursts into action, and the words come on the screen: 'A glass and a half full of – *no not milk (which used to be what they put in Cadbury's chocolate)* - 'A glass and a half full of **JOY**!'

Passions, emotions, happiness, ecstasy, pleasurable feelings, exhilaration - these are the words and ideas the world uses to describe joy, whether it's the joy of playing the drums, the promise of a bar of chocolate, your team winning a crucial match, or joy at the birth of a baby, or at the sight of spring lambs, or a glorious sunset. But I am not sure that these words and ideas quite capture the meaning of joy here in this description of the fruit of the Spirit.

There are something like 11 different Greek words reflecting various aspects of joy, yet in Galatians 5:22 there is, of course, just one word - *chara*

What does this word mean? At the simplest level it does mean 'gladness, delight'. But it does not mean being silly, or irresponsible, flippant or facetious in expressing such delight or gladness.

'Gladness/delight' are not the same as 'happiness'. Most of the worldly definitions of 'joy' relate more to aspects of happiness, but happiness depends on circumstances; joy doesn't. Happiness is experienced when outward conditions are favourable, to our liking, and we seek happiness by trying to create favourable conditions, sometimes in misguided ways.

Happiness does not last; it is ephemeral, short-lived, which is why we feel the need to keep pursuing it. Joy – the kind Paul has in mind here – is deep and lasting regardless of circumstances.

What then is joy? Matthew Henry describes joy as *a constant delight in God.* This means seeing God as the source of all good gifts, in the past, present and future, seeing God as in control in all circumstances and at all times. *A constant delight in God* - that's what joy is.

But in this dark world what reasons do we have to rejoice? People are dying of starvation, there's fighting, conflict, injustice, poverty, hatred, natural disasters, tragic accidents, selfishness, greed, appalling acts of violence, and now in 2020/2021, a pandemic that is overwhelming even the wealthier and more advanced nations of the world, and yet we know this is not the whole story. Even in the midst of all this darkness and wickedness and tragedy, we can look and see God's many gifts in the world around us.

On at least one occasion, Paul reminded his young friend Timothy that **God richly provides us with everything for our enjoyment.** Are we going to deny this? Are we going to let all the negative aspects of life and society rob us of the many things God has given us for our enjoyment?

For example, we can rejoice in the world of nature, the sights and sounds of the world, colours, songs of the birds, textures, the roughness (or smoothness sometimes) in the bark of trees, and rocks and stones. A cooling breeze on a hot sticky day, refreshing rain restoring life to our gardens and the countryside, the smell of spring, of new mown hay, hedgerows, wayside flowers, the dampness of rich leaf mould in woodland - all there to enjoy!

I am reminded of a poem I placed at the beginning of my ebook of sermons called 'In The Beginning':-

*I thank You, God, that I have lived
In this great world and known its many joys;
The song of birds, the strong, sweet scent of hay,
and cooling breezes in the secret dusk,
The flaming sunsets at the close of the day,
hills, and the lonely, heather-covered moors,
Music at night, and moonlight on the sea,
the beat of waves upon the rocky shore
and wild, white spray, flung high in ecstasy:
The faithful eyes of dogs, and treasured books.
The love of kin and fellowship of friends,
and all that makes life dear and beautiful.
I thank You, too, that there has come to me
a little sorrow and, sometimes, defeat,
A little heartache and the loneliness
that comes with parting,
and the word 'Goodbye,'
Dawn breaking after dreary hours of pain,
when I discovered that night's gloom must yield
And morning light breaks through to me again.
Because of these and other blessings poured,
unasked upon my wondering head,
Because I know that there is yet to come
an even richer and more glorious life,
And most of all, because Your only Son
once sacrificed life's loveliness for me
– I thank You, God, that I have lived.*
(Elizabeth Craven)

I thank You, God, that I have lived in this great world and known its many joys

In Psalm 92 verse 4 we read ***For you make me glad, O Lord; I sing for joy at the work of your hands...***

It has been said that we need to go through this world with our 'eyes wide, our nostrils dilated and our ears open so that we can recognise and rejoice in God's creation'.

If joy is part of the fruit of the Spirit, then we need to ask the Holy Spirit to show us the Father's world and create a new awareness and joy and delight in the 'work of God's hands'.

We can, then, rejoice in the natural world, God's creation. And we can rejoice in the everyday gifts of God as he supplies all our needs, material, emotional, and social. Food and shelter and clothing, families and friends, Christian fellowship, a sense of God's presence, times of special help received, even the swings and roundabouts of our emotions. These are all God's gifts and we can rejoice in them.

And we can, of course, rejoice in God's greatest gift – his Son Jesus Christ. We can rejoice at his coming into this world. Remember the angels' song of good news of great joy announced at his birth? We can rejoice that in Christ God has lived this human life with all its varied experiences. We can rejoice at Christ's teachings, remembering that joy was often a characteristic of so much of Christ's teaching.

In Luke 15, by means of three parables, we are shown the joy of finding that which was lost. There are also the parables of the hidden treasure and the pearl of great price, which are mainly about the joy of finding something of great value.

We can rejoice at Christ's obedience, his willingness to die in obedience to the Father's will and for our sakes. We can rejoice in the Easter story. Have you ever noticed how prominent joy is in the gospel accounts of the first

Easter?. Matthew 28:8 ***The women hurried away from the tomb, afraid YET FILLED WITH JOY***
Luke 24:41 ***Jesus showed them his hands and feet and they still did not believe it because of JOY and amazement***

And after the Ascension, Luke 24:52 ***They returned to Jerusalem WITH GREAT JOY***

We can rejoice because Christ came into the world, and we can rejoice in our spiritual condition as a result of his incarnation, death and resurrection, for not only has Christ come into the world, but also into our lives here and now in the 21st century.

Romans 5:1 ***Therefore, since we have been justified through faith, we have peace with God through our Lord Jesus Christ...*** and v 11 ***We rejoice in God through our Lord Jesus Christ through whom we are reconciled.***

We are justified by faith, we have peace with God, we are reconciled – these are descriptions of our spiritual condition. **Justification** is a book-keeping term; it means God has taken the sum total of all the terrible things I've done in life - all the sins ever committed that are set out there against my name in the ledger - and he has transferred them all and set them against the name of Christ.

Not only this, not only has he transferred all my debts, but he has transferred all the goodness, righteousness of Christ to my account. All the bad stuff to Christ; all the goodness to me.

If you were to have a credit card and run up a few hundred or thousand pounds of debt, and someone legally transferred your debt to his account, and then transferred money from his account into yours, so that instead of owing thousands of pounds, you had now received thousands, wouldn't you rejoice? I think I might!

But God isn't dealing with money. He deals with something far more important - life! Eternal life! A lasting relationship with almighty God! And we are meant to enjoy it!

I know it cost Christ his life, I know that is very serious, but we are encouraged to rejoice in our new status as God's children, bought at great cost and dearly loved.

Our future prospects are also further cause for joy. Romans 5:2 *we rejoice in the hope of the glory of God*

Hope is an aspect of Christian joy. A text often seen on war memorials reminds us that joy and hope are related - *sorrow not as those who have no hope.* Sorrow is for those who have no hope; joy is for those with sure and certain hope in God. It's about the future, and when we think what the future holds for those who belong to Christ, this is surely cause for joy and gladness.

Whatever the precise details of the return of Christ, and the day of judgement, Paul says – *since we have now been justified by his blood, how much more shall we be saved from God's wrath through him!*

Hope speaks of our eternal destiny in the everlasting presence of God, eternal safety, security, peace, fellowship with God and one another.

So, we can rejoice in the future, and because of this we can rejoice in the present even in the midst of suffering! Remember that joy means a constant delight in God independent of outward circumstances.

Billy Graham tells of his father-in-law returning from China where his young son had been buried, and this grieving father wrote 'There are tears in our eyes but there is joy in our hearts' - joy in grief and suffering.

Amy Carmichael was a missionary in India during the first half of the last century. In 1931 she fell and as result was crippled with arthritis and bed-ridden for last 20 years of her life, during which time she wrote many books. It is said that 'joy filled her sick room so that everyone who visited her came away praising God' - joy even in suffering.

We can rejoice in what God has done in the past, rejoice in what is yet to come, but the period in between is also a time for joy and gladness.

Stuart Briscoe (a Keswick speaker) says... *Sometimes our spiritual position is like an old bedstead - rock steady at each end but inclined to sag in the middle. Our future is assured, our past has already happened, the problem is often in the middle, the here and now.*

It is because of the past and the future that we can find joy even in our sufferings, and the reason Paul gives in Romans 5 is because present suffering can be creative. Suffering produces perseverance and perseverance produces character, and character produces hope.

There are so many reasons to rejoice despite the negativity I keep seeing in Christian newsletters and online messages at the moment. There is, despite the pandemic we've been living through for the past 9-10 months, much cause for joy and gladness in our lives, and the word of God instructs us... ***Rejoice in the Lord always - rejoice!***

Rejoice - not just if you feel like it. Rejoice in the Lord **always**! And perhaps we should add 'all ways'. Our reply may well be 'we can't!' Of course we can't. If we could, it wouldn't be listed here as part of the fruit of Spirit! We depend on the Holy Spirit to produce this fruit, and we encourage production by living Christ-centred, Spirit-controlled lives!

What's the good old children's song? *'Joy is the flag flown high from the castle of my heart'.* When? *'When the King is in residence there'*

It's been said that joy is the most infallible sign of the presence of God, a sign that the King of kings is in residence in our hearts and lives.

There are many things in which to rejoice. Indeed, when we stop and think about it, it ought to be harder to be miserable than to rejoice! But this depends on the presence of God in the heart of a Christian believer.

Let St Francis of Assisi have the final word: *Let us leave sadness to the devil and his angels. As for us, what can we be but rejoicing and glad?*

Chapter Four

The fruit of the Spirit is… peace

Here are some news reports from this past week *(October 2008)…*

- *"The latest US defence department report on the situation in Iraq says the fundamental character of the conflict in Iraq remains unchanged, despite dramatic security improvements there. Iraq remains locked in a communal struggle for power and resources. The report identifies Iran's influence as the major long-term security threat. 'Despite continued Iranian promises to the contrary, it appears clear that Iran continues to fund, train, arm, and direct special groups intent on destabilising the situation in Iraq,'"*

- *"Security sources in north Lebanon say two more people have died of their wounds from last Monday's bomb explosion. The deaths take the number of those killed in the incident to seven. It is not clear who carried out the attack, which targeted an army bus in Tripoli. Earlier, the parliamentary majority leader denounced Syria's president for saying Tripoli and north Lebanon had become a base for extremists."*

- *"A pilotless American drone has fired missiles in a border area of Pakistan, killing at least four people. Officials said a house was hit near the town of Mir Ali in North Waziristan and nine people were injured. Tension between the US and Pakistan has increased over cross-border incursions against militants by American military based in Afghanistan."*

- *"A Hindu woman has been killed as police have tried to control more violence between Christians and Hindus in the eastern Indian state of Orissa. They say that the violence began in the state's Kandhamal district when a Hindu mob attacked a Christian priest. Police say that the priest's son retaliated by firing on the crowd, leading to further clashes. Orissa has seen weeks of anti-Christian violence. Correspondents say it is caused by ethnic and religious tension. Over 30 people have been killed in the violence and thousands forced to flee their homes and seek shelter in relief camps."*

All this was taking place in just one region of the world., and there are, of course, many other conflicts across the world. It's right therefore that we should pray for peace, but what do we mean when we say that?

When we say that we long and pray for peace in the Middle East, in Iraq, in other parts of the world, we are usually expressing a longing for an end to all the hostility and hatred and violence, but the Bible has a much broader concept of peace. According to the Bible, conflict, hatred, hostility, disunity, violence are themselves just symptoms of the absence of peace, but peace itself is not understood simply as being an absence of conflict. The Biblical concept is much broader than this.

For example, do you remember how, Judges 6, Gideon was threshing wheat in a winepress? We may not realise this but a winepress wasn't the usual place for threshing wheat. I'm not quite sure why but winepresses were usually sunk into the ground. This is certainly the impression we get from the parable Jesus told in Matthew 21:- ***there was a landowner who planted a vineyard. He put a wall round it, dug a winepress in it and built a watchtower. Then he rented the vineyard to some farmers and moved to another place.*** *(Matt*

21:33). So Gideon was actually hiding down there, afraid that the Midianites would come and steal the wheat. The Lord comes up behind Gideon and says (with a touch of irony) ***The Lord is with you, mighty warrior!***

I suspect that the last thing Gideon felt like was a mighty warrior! After all, he's hiding in the winepress. The Lord continued though and told Gideon to do all kinds of interesting things like - ***Go and knock down your father's altar to Baal; kill your father's prize bull; chop down the Asherah pole*** (a symbol of the pagan goddess Asherah), ***build another altar to the Lord, sacrifice the bull on it; and while you're at it - declare war on the Midianites.***

Eventually Gideon was persuaded to do all this, by means of various signs given to him. And then what did he do? Gideon built an altar to the Lord and called it ***Jehovah-Shalom - The Lord is Peace***

The last thing Gideon was going to experience with this God-given agenda was going to be an absence of conflict. He wasn't ending a war, for example. He was starting one! He wasn't opting for a quiet easy life. His obedience to the Lord's instructions were going to provoke an angry reaction from his own people and in particular, his own father.

Gideon, however. understood what real peace was, and that it was related to God, and doing God's will. His own life was about to be plunged into total chaos, turned upside down, but he trusted that God knew what he was doing and that in trustful obedience Gideon would find peace.

If our concept of peace is confined to the absence of hostility, tension, pressure in our lives, we are going to be very disappointed because we will never get rid of tension and conflict in this life, especially as followers of Jesus. Jesus calls his followers to walk the way of the cross. He sent his disciples out as sheep among wolves.

But Jesus also said, *My peace I give you*, which suggests that his peace is not the kind the world knows. In John 16:33, Jesus said, *I have told you these things so that in me you may have peace. In this world you will have trouble. But take heart! I have overcome the world.* All of this suggests that the peace the Holy Spirit is trying to create in our lives is not peace as the world understands it.

Augustine, the North African theologian of the 4th and 5th centuries AD defines peace as *the tranquillity of order*, and that word 'order' is the key to understanding the Biblical concept of *peace.*

One commentator offers a clumsy but fairly memorable phrase: *Peace is the consequence of a life ordered according to the orders of the God of order.* Put more simply, peace comes from living in obedience to the will of God.

In practical terms this is about our relationships being ordered according to the orders of the God of order. We can see this is three distinct areas of life: our relationship with God, with others, and with ourselves.

The Holy Spirit is God's agent for peace; he looks at all the chaos and disorder in our lives and in the world and he longs to bring order, peace. In Genesis 1:1,2 we read - *In the beginning God created the heavens and the earth. Now the earth was formless and empty, darkness was over the surface of the deep, and the Spirit of God was hovering over the waters.* Why was the Spirit of God 'hovering over the waters'? Because he was longing to bring order to this empty, formless mass.

One of the laws of thermodynamics says that things tend towards a state of disorder unless acted upon by an outside force. It may be a law of thermodynamics, but it also seems to be a law of nature as any gardener will tell you. *Things tend towards a state of disorder unless acted upon by an outside force.* It seems also to be a law of life too. Life, relationships especially, degenerate into a state of chaos and disorder unless acted upon by an outside force, and the Spirit of God is a powerful and effective force bringing peace into our lives, or rather, for the believer, the Holy Spirit isn't an <u>outside</u> force; he works from within.

First of all the Holy Spirit works in the area of our **relationship with God.**

As humans we have been created with a spiritual awareness; it's part of who we are. We are spiritual beings as well as earthly, physical beings. This means we have the ability to think beyond what we see and touch and taste and sense in this material world. We are spiritual beings, but our spiritual awareness is so easily perverted. The result is disorder, confusion in people's thinking about God.

Many people know there's something wrong in their lives. They have a sense that life isn't quite as it should be, that something is missing. This is a sign of our spiritual awareness. Just look in bookshops, gift shops, market stalls and you will see signs of this awareness of a spiritual dimension in life. Psychic fairs are another sign of this awareness. The current interest in 'mindfulness' is another sign. The problem is that people have a tendency to go looking for answers in the wrong places, such as astrology, Eastern religions, (and even some primitive western religions nowadays), crystals, other religious artefacts, but these only lead to even greater chaos and confusion in people's minds. We can only have peace with God through Jesus Christ.

The Holy Spirit works to bring us this peace long before ever we realise it, as he creates this hunger, and an awareness that all is not well, that there must be something more to life. The Spirit also aims to bring about what we term 'conviction' of sin, an awareness of our sinful nature. And then, given the opportunity, the Holy Spirit guides us towards the answer, Jesus Christ.

We cannot have peace with God other than through Jesus Christ. In Acts of the Apostles, we read how Peter told Cornelius of '***the good news of peace through Jesus Christ, who is Lord of all'.*** In Romans 5:1 Paul says '***we have peace with God through our Lord Jesus Christ'***. In Ephesians 2... '***But now in Christ Jesus you who were once far away have been brought near through the blood of Christ. For he himself is our peace'.*** In Colossians 1 Paul refers to God making '***peace through Christ's blood, shed on the cross'.***

Peace with God, a right relationship with God, this is the work of the Holy Spirit. But we need to understand this. That this peace does not always come gently. Quite often the Holy Spirit needs to confront certain aspects of our lives. He may need to battle against anything and everything that shuts God out of any part of our lives, anything and everything that threatens to disrupt our relationship with God. The Holy Spirit may need to disturb us and turn our lives upside down, but he does this so that we can have peace with God.

The Holy Spirit is also working to create peace in our **relationships with other people.**

The New Testament is full of references to living at peace with one another. I am not going to list them now. You can look them up in a concordance or online.

We have many words which denote a lack of peace and order in our relationships with others: disunity, discord, disharmony, division, resentment, bitterness, envy and jealousy, hatred, strife. These are all symptoms of an absence of peace in our relationships with other people.

There is also disorder in international relationships fuelled by the greed and self-interest of nations. There's disorder in society, disorder in families and, sadly, disorder in our churches, and all because there's an absence of peace caused by relationships that are not *ordered according to the orders of the God of order.*

The Holy Spirit is working to create peace in this area of our lives, in our relationships with other people, but he needs our cooperation if it's going to happen. He needs a willingness to shift our focus in life away from ourselves to other people and their needs.

The third area in which the Holy Spirit is working to create peace is in our **relationship with ourselves**

The Holy Spirit wants to take away disorder and confusion and stress in our personal lives, and give us peace with ourselves.

We are strange creatures, we humans! We seem to have dual personalities. We have a capacity for standing apart from ourselves. Sometimes we are very good at looking at ourselves and being critical, sometimes we can become frustrated or disappointed with ourselves. It's as if we are able to stand aside and observe ourselves.

We see Paul doing just this in Romans 7 – he says... *I don't understand it. For what I want to do I do not do. But what I hate I do.* Paul speaks of two forces at work within him, and in various ways we all have this internal conflict, this civil war going on within us.

Sometimes this conflict within ourselves leads to confusion and a feeling of helplessness. It's as if there's a force at work which we are unable to control. Or as Scripture puts it: *'The spirit is willing but the flesh is weak'*

The result is that we become unhappy, depressed, in some ways even hating ourselves. We put ourselves down, we see ourselves as having little or no value. This isn't how it's meant to be. The problem then is that, instead of shifting the focus away from ourselves, our inner dissatisfaction and frustration and unhappiness can make us focus more on ourselves.

The Holy Spirit's aim is to take this frustration and unhappiness, confusion, tension, and in its place, create peace with ourselves.

Of course, Jesus calls his disciples to deny self and acknowledge his Lordship over our lives. The hymn, *Lord for the years* includes these words:
Lord, for ourselves, in living power remake us
- self on the cross and Christ upon the throne

There is that need for self-denial and the recognition of Christ's Lordship over our lives, but at the same time this does not mean belittling ourselves.

Graham Kendrick wrote a song for children but it contains a truth that we all should take to heart:
I'm special because God has loved me,
For he gave the best thing that he had to save me

The Holy Spirit comes reminding us that we, every one of us, is special. God sent his Son into the world for our sakes. Doesn't that suggest we're special to God? Christ died for us. We are God's children, children of the King of kings, and therefore princes and princesses! And when we've really begun to grasp what this means, then the Holy Spirit has begun to create peace with ourselves.

The fruit of the Spirit is, among other things **peace.** The Holy Spirit longs to create order in our confused, disorderly lives. So *why doesn't he?* Because, as always, he needs our co-operation. Certain conditions are needed if this fruit is going to be produced in our lives.

The first is this: **trust**

Gideon had to trust that God knew best, and it was because he trusted God that Gideon was able to say '*The Lord is Peace*'. We have to trust that God is committed, totally committed, to bringing peace and order, harmony and wholeness to our lives. He is absolutely committed to guiding us through this life and into the next. God is completely dedicated to working for our good, and even if he turns our lives upside down or inside out, we need to trust that, if we *order our lives according to the orders of the God of order*, then chaos and confusion will not be the long-term result. And where, instead of peace, we have fears and worries, then the reason is that we are not trusting God.

There is a simple little poem that goes like this:
Said the robin to the sparrow,
'I should really like to know
Why these anxious human beings
Rush around and worry so.'

Said the sparrow to the robin,
'Friend, I think that it must be
That they have no Heavenly Father
Such as cares for you and me'

Well, we **do** have a heavenly Father who, through Christ, says that we are worth more than many sparrows!

Along with trust we need something else. As the old hymn says, we need to trust **and** obey. Disobedience leads to disorder in our lives and relationships. Isaiah 48:18 speaks of *peace like a river*, and how do we have such peace? Here's the whole quotation from Isaiah 48 - **If only you had paid attention to my commands** *(been obedient, allowed your life and relationships to be ordered by my orders)* **your peace would have been like a river.**

Those who pay no attention to God's commands and therefore no attention to God's ways can expect confusion and disorder in their lives. Those who disregard the teachings of scripture concerning the way we should treat one another can expect to reap a harvest of disharmony and division. The root cause of so much disorder in today's world is disobedience and an utter disregard for God and the way of life set out for us in and through Jesus Christ.

Philippians 4:6 ***Do not be anxious about anything, but in everything, by prayer and petition, with thanksgiving, present your requests to God...*** Paul says do this ***and the PEACE OF GOD, which transcends all understanding, will guard your hearts and your minds in Christ Jesus.***

Trust, Obey, and Pray and the Holy Spirit will find it so much easier to create the 'tranquillity of order' in your life and relationships.

Drop thy still dews of quietness
till all our strivings cease;
take from our souls the strain and stress,
and let our <u>ordered</u> lives confess
the beauty of thy peace.

Chapter Five

The fruit of the Spirit is… patience.

The Fruit of the Spirit provides us with a description of what a mature Christian looks like in terms of personality and character. You see, Christian maturity doesn't necessarily just come with age, with the passing of years.

There was this woman waiting patiently in her Mercedes car, waiting patiently for a parking place to become vacant. The shopping centre was busy. She'd spent quite some time going round and round, searching for a parking space. Suddenly she spotted a man laden down with shopping bags and heading for his car. She drove up, parked behind him and waited while he loaded his car. Eventually he got into his car and reversed out of the space. But before the woman in the Mercedes could drive into the parking space, a young man in a flashy new sports car nipped round her and occupied the empty space. He opened the door and got out of his car, and with a flourish he zapped his car with his remote control and started walking away.

'Hey!' shouted the woman in the Mercedes. 'I've been waiting ages for that parking space!'
'Sorry, lady.' said the young man. 'That's how it is when you're young and quick!'

With that she put her Mercedes in gear, put her foot hard on the accelerator and ran her car into the back of the sports car, twisting the rear bumper out of shape and denting a corner panel.

The young man came running back shouting, 'You can't do that!'
'Sorry, young man,' said the lady in the Mercedes. 'But that's how it is when you're old and rich!'

I suspect that those of us who are older but probably not rich are tempted to say 'Good for you!', but the story does illustrate the truth that maturity does not necessarily come with age. You can be young and foolish, and you can just as easily be old and foolish, and the fruit of the Spirit is about the Holy Spirit working to make sure we are neither but that regardless of age, we become mature Christians.

The fruit of the Spirit is love, joy, peace, and <u>patience.</u>

Patience is something many of us would say we could do with a bit more of, but what do we mean by that? What is 'patience'?

The dictionary says patience is…

- *the calm endurance of pain*
- *forbearance*
- *perseverance*
- *a quiet and self-possessed spirit*
- *waiting for something*
- *a card game, usually played by one person!*

Of course, here in Galatians 5 the original word is not English but Greek – *makrothumia*. It means *to be long-tempered.* The Hebrew equivalent of the Greek word in the Old Testament means not long *tempered* but long *nostrils*. To be patient is to have long nostrils! What does that mean? - 'the fruit of the Spirit is *long nostrils'?*

We don't often come across the word 'nostril' in the Bible, but if we take a concordance and look up the word to see if there are any Bible references using the word, we do indeed find the word 'nostrils' in Psalm 18:7-8 - ***The earth trembled and quaked, and the foundations of the mountains shook; they trembled because God was angry. Smoke rose from <u>his nostrils</u>*** and then later in v 15 - ***The valleys of the sea were exposed and the foundations of the earth laid bare at your rebuke - at the <u>blast of breath from your nostrils</u>***

The idea is that of anger being expressed through the nostrils. I suppose the idea is of intense breathing through the nose, like the snorting of an angry bull.

But why **long** nostrils? It suggests the anger taking a long time coming out, before being expressed. In other words, to be patient means 'slow to anger'. That's the Hebrew idea of patience - slow to anger.

The Greek word, *makrothumia* is a composite of two words: *makro* meaning 'long' and *thumia* meaning 'temper'. 'Long-tempered'. But have you ever come across such an expression? I haven't, so I looked in the dictionary again, but the word or expression wasn't there. On the other hand, 'short-tempered' is and this is a more familiar expression describing someone who is quick to express anger. They have a 'short fuse', we say. To be patient then is the opposite of 'short-tempered', **slow** to anger, having a **long** fuse rather than a short one.

Notice though that being 'slow to anger' doesn't rule out the possibility of being angry. It simply allows time for the anger to dissipate.

Anger can be a bit of a problem for some of us. It isn't simply the fact that we recognise anger as being a part of life. It's that we don't feel very comfortable with the idea of being angry; we have a sense that anger is wrong. We have the feeling that we heard that somewhere, and we did! The 'somewhere' is Matthew 5:22 where Jesus said: ***I tell you that anyone who is <u>angry</u> with his brother will be subject to judgement.***

If you have good eyesight you will see that the NIV has a footnote for this verse saying *some mss add 'without cause'* so we can read verse 22 as ***anyone who is <u>angry</u> with his brother <u>without cause</u> will be subject to judgement,*** but it is no use grasping at that straw because the consensus of Bible scholars suggest that 'without cause' is a later addition to those manuscripts.

The problem remains then. Patience means 'slow to anger' which doesn't rule out the possibility of being angry. And the apostle Paul seems to support this in Ephesians 4:26 where, quoting Psalm 4, he writes ***In your anger do not sin*** yet Jesus says ***'anyone who is angry with his brother will be subject to judgement'.*** Are we allowed to be angry or not?

The answer lies in the fact that there are two kinds of anger. The Bible shows us that sometimes God is an angry God! We don't like to be reminded of this but it's a fact. We don't like to hear about the wrath of God, but anger is as much a part of God's character as love, joy, peace and so forth.

God's anger is absolutely necessary if he is going to be a **just** God. If God is going to stand for what is right, then he will need to demonstrate how firmly he stands for what is right by the way he reacts against what is wrong. If sin and evil, injustice, cruelty are not met with an angry response from God, it could suggest that they don't really matter.

God's anger is absolutely necessary if he is going to be a **loving** God. A loving father will express anger towards a wayward child. To be over-tolerant, indulgent, turning a blind eye is not the action of a loving parent!

God's love is sometimes expressed through anger. The Old Testament prophets used strong words to warn God's people and others concerning impending doom, judgement. But such words of warning are words spoken by a loving, but angry, Father seeking to turn the hearts of his wayward children.

God's anger is not like ours. We must not make the mistake of thinking of human anger and then enlarging it and saying this is God's anger. Human anger can be right and proper yet very unfair, and it always arises from incomplete knowledge, which means we won't always get it right. God is holy which, among other things means that he is different, and righteous, and just and true in all his ways. God has complete knowledge, and perfect wisdom, and therefore God's anger is always just and loving, and determined by perfect wisdom and truth. And it's slow!

The fact that we are still here living on earth and not in heaven, the fact that Christ has not yet returned, and that the history books have not yet closed, and the final day of judgement is not upon us - all these are sure signs that God is patient, slow to anger. After all, God has every reason to be angry as he looks on the world today. He has every reason to pull down the final curtain, but he is patient, slow to anger.

God's anger is holy, just, loving and slow. This is one kind of anger, and we call it ***righteous*** anger, but there is another kind of anger which, as you might have guessed, is ***unrighteous anger.*** God's anger is always under his control, but unrighteous anger is uncontrolled anger, and it's the kind of anger Jesus was referring to in the verse from the sermon on the mount. Uncontrolled anger is dangerous because we do not know where it might lead.

When Jesus said - ***'anyone who is angry with his brother will be subject to judgement'***, he had first quoted the law... 'Do not murder - anyone who murders will be subject to judgement', and his warning was a warning against the kind of anger that is murder in embryonic form. This is the kind of anger that can so easily get out of hand, so easily go too far, anger rooted in hatred and contempt.

Nowhere in the Bible will you find this kind of anger either encouraged or permitted.

Unrighteous anger is uncontrolled anger, and it's also self-centred anger. More often than not our anger, whether we manage to contain it inwardly or express it outwardly has a tendency to be self-centred.

Someone offends us, or we feel we aren't getting the attention and recognition we think we ought to have, so what happens? The anger wells up within us until we have an angry outburst to make sure people listen to us.

Perhaps our needs are being overlooked, or our self-esteem has taken a battering through a word of criticism, so we get angry.

Sometimes others may be at fault and we may have some cause for complaint, but it's still self-centred anger, anger that's about 'me', my feelings, my rights, my needs.

There are then two kinds of anger – righteous anger and unrighteous anger.

Jesus himself was angry on occasions. He was certainly displeased when he saw that the temple precincts had been turned into a marketplace. He was angry at this desecration of his Father's house, and the exploitation of people, and dishonest practices.

We read in Mark 3 that Jesus was angry with those who tried to find fault in his healing on the Sabbath.

He called the scribes and Pharisees 'blind fools!' because of their unbelief and opposition concerning the unfolding of the kingdom of God, and the will and purposes of God being expressed through Christ. Was this righteous anger or unrighteous anger?

Jesus burned with indignation and anger at sin, injustice, unbelief, oppression and exploitation, but his own ego was never wrapped up in the issue. Indeed, when he was unjustly arrested, unfairly tried, illegally beaten, spat upon, crucified, mocked and when he had every reason to burn with anger and indignation, how did Jesus respond? Peter tells us ***When they hurled insults at Jesus, he did not retaliate; when he suffered, he made***

no threats. Instead, from his parched lips, as he hung on the cross, Jesus said ***Father, forgive them, for they do not know what they are doing***

Righteous anger is perfectly demonstrated in the person of Jesus Christ.

By contrast, when we suffer personal attack, we can be very quick to express anger, we can be very impatient, and yet we can be very patient when we see injustice, and attacks on the dignity and rights and reputations of others!

The fruit of the Spirit is patience but I've spent most of this chapter talking about anger! This is because patience is about being slow to anger, and understanding what anger is all about helps us to understand and appreciate God's ***patience*** and what patience means for us.

God is very patient with us, isn't he? God has demonstrated incredible patience with each one of us. We can be slow to understand and accept His truth revealed in Christ Jesus, yet he remains patient. For all our wrongdoing, God still accepts us. He sees our disobedience, our slowness to respond to his call, our reluctance to speak a word for him, yet still he goes on loving and caring and working out his purposes in and through us.

God is very patient with us, and he expects the same from us! That's what the parable of the Unmerciful Servant is all about.

This person owed the king millions of pounds, and he falls on his knees before the king, and begs the king to be patient with him and he will pay back everything he owes (even though he had no hope of ever being able to do this). The king cancelled the debt. But as the story continues, it seems someone owed this person some money and made the same plea: *Be patient with me! I will pay back everything.* But the plea is rejected. The king learns of this and brings the first person to justice.

God expects us also to be patient since he shows great patience towards us.

People have all kinds of messages on tee-shirts. I recall one that said *Be patient with me - God's not finished with me yet!* We could all do with making that same plea! *Be patient with me - God's not finished with me yet!* as a reminder to be patient, slow to anger, with one another, a reminder to remember how patient God is with us and how we too should treat one another in similar fashion.

Patience is part of the fruit of the Spirit, the result of the Holy Spirit working in our lives. It's another way in which the Holy Spirit is seeking to reproduce God's character in his children. Impatience is a sign for all to see, an indication that we are not allowing the Holy Spirit to work in us and change us. We betray ourselves, we betray the truth about ourselves when we are impatient.

One last comment. This aspect of the fruit of the Spirit will not appear, develop, grow, mature in the <u>absence</u> of trials, affliction, opposition, suffering, provocation. Patience does not grow in a vacuum.

I heard the story when I was a child about a man who had been reading the early chapters of Joshua, and he had been struck by the words 'Be strong and courageous' which come four times in Joshua 1. So this man prayed to God: 'Make me strong and courageous'.

The next day a lion escaped from a visiting circus, and the man came face to face with this lion in the middle of the street, which wasn't quite what the man had expected when he set out from his home that day. It was, however, an opportunity to find out whether or not the prayer had been answered!

I'm sorry but I don't know what the outcome was! But

the story illustrates an important truth, that when we pray that God will grant us this gift of patience, making us long-tempered, slow to anger, then in answering our prayer God may need to place us in circumstances or, more than likely, in the company of those who will teach us something of the meaning of patience, and in that way he will provide the opportunity to exercise this new gift!

Chapter Six

The fruit of the Spirit is... kindness

The Russian author Tolstoy tells the story of a shoemaker who was going home one night after a hard day's work, and he saw a stranger standing shivering in a church doorway. This stranger was dressed in what can only be described as dirty rags. The shoemaker took the stranger home. His wife complained at first: *'What did you want to bring him home for? Haven't we got little enough for ourselves without another mouth to feed? And look at him - he's dirty. Goodness knows what parasites and diseases he's brought with him!'* So she complained and nagged and as she continued, the stranger grew smaller and smaller. With every unkind word, he seemed to grow more wrinkled and thinner, whereas when she managed to find the grace to speak pleasantly and give him food, he grew more and more beautiful. Why? 'Because,' says Tolstoy. 'The stranger was an angel who had fallen from heaven and who could not live except in an atmosphere of love and kindness.

A little boy came rushing into the house one day, carrying a bunch of flowers which he had gathered for his mother. He was only a very young boy and didn't know that a bit of golden rod and willow herb gathered from the dusty wasteland nearby didn't have much value. His mother was out but his sister was there. She saw her little brother clutching his gift and she just laughed at him and said *'Mum won't think much of those - they're horrible!'* The boy's face dropped, he went outside and threw his precious offering in the dustbin.

What tremendous power God has entrusted to us! God has entrusted us with a power that can destroy people or build them up, and kindness is one of the ways we exercise this power.

What does 'kindness' mean?

The dictionary defines kindness as: 'the actions of a sympathetic, forbearing, gentle, pleasant nature.' The Hebrew word for 'kindness' is the word *chesed* which literally means '*to treat courteously and appropriately*'. It is also translated in the Old Testament as *'loving-kindness.'* The Greek word is *chrestotes* which literally means *'useful, pleasant, gracious.'* but the translators of the King James Bible translate this word as '*gentleness.*'

In his book about the fruit of the Spirit, Stephen Winward writes: *'Kindness includes sympathy, generosity and benevolence.'* Another Christian writer - Philip Keller – writes - *Kindness involves finding ways to 'brighten and cheer' the lives of others.*

Putting all this together then, kindness is *'caring enough about others that we treat them with gentleness, graciousness and generosity as we find ways to 'brighten and cheer' their lives.'*

In this chapter we are going to think about various characteristics of kindness. For example, kindness is not just about what we do, but the way we are. It has something to do with a person's nature or personality, and the manner in which we carry out so-called ***acts of kindness.***

Secondly, kindness includes **courtesy**, which in turn means consideration shown towards others.

Some of the books on my shelves belong to a bygone age and can therefore seem quaint and old-fashioned in today's world, but this does not make their words or wisdom any less valid. In one such book I read this, a father's advice to his son. *'Son, treat everyone with politeness, even those who are rude to you; for remember, you show courtesy to others not because **they** are gentlemen, but because **you** are a gentleman.'* This may seem a bit old-fashioned but I believe it contains a sound principle that we do well to follow (or the equivalent, if you are a lady!)

Kindness then includes courtesy and consideration.

Thirdly, a kind person is an **approachable** person, someone to whom we can turn for help and advice, someone we can turn to without fear of being rebuffed, snubbed, rudely rejected.

Fourthly, kindness is **indiscriminate** and **inclusive**. After all, surely it would be **un**kind to differentiate between people on account of race, or age, or sex, or riches, status, or occupation, or where they come from, or which part of the town they live in.

Fifthly, a kind person is a **mellow** person. In Luke 5:39 Jesus said *No one after drinking old wine wants the new for he says 'The old is better'* and the word 'better' is the Greek word usually translated as 'kind', or 'kinder'. *The old is <u>kinder</u>* - more mellow.

What else can we say about kindness? In Matthew 11 Jesus says *My yoke is easy and my burden is light,* and there the word 'easy' is the same word translated elsewhere as 'kind'. In that context the word refers to the yoke on a beast of burden, and this master carpenter, Jesus, might well be quoting his advertising slogan written across the door of his workshop: *'My yoke is easy'.* It is kind to your animals, it will not chafe.

Kind people do not chafe! They do not irritate or deliberately make us feel uncomfortable. The truly kind person does not even cause the discomfort of embarrassing others by their kindness.

Seventhly, Campbell-Morgan suggests kindness is helpfulness in small things, and this ensures that acts of kindness are motivated by love and nothing else. Back in 1985 it was very kind of Bob Geldof to be so moved by the plight of millions of starving people in Africa that he organised Live Aid. I believe he was sincere and not seeking publicity to further his own career, although it didn't do him any harm in that respect!

Comic Relief is another way in which many comedians raise money to help people in desperate need, but after its initial sincerity, we can't be absolutely sure that participants are motivated only by love.

People do all kinds of things to raise money for Children In Need and their efforts are commendable, but there is also publicity and kudos for those taking part.

Those little acts of kindness, on the other hand, that often go unheralded, unnoticed, unrecognised are motivated first and foremost by love and by the Holy Spirit.

Kindness is about the willingness to do simple little things to help other people. Jesus said that the simple act of giving a cup of cold water to someone does not go unnoticed in heaven, it costs little or nothing, but its essentially about seeing the need and meeting it.

This leads on to the eight characteristic of kindness. Sensitivity to people's needs, being thoughtful.

In previous chapters, each of the aspects of the fruit of the Spirit reflects an aspect of God's character. The love, joy, peace, patience that the Holy Spirit aims to create in our lives is the same love, joy, peace and patience we see in God himself, and I'm sure no one would argue when we say the same here. It's God's kindness that the Holy Spirit is endeavouring to reproduce in our lives.

In Psalm 34:8 we find those familiar words - ***Taste and see that the Lord is good.*** The word translated 'good' there is actually the word meaning 'kind'. '***Taste and see that the Lord is <u>kind</u>***. In the previous chapter I suggested that 'patience' means 'slow to anger', and God is slow to anger not only because of his patience but because of his kindness. God prefers to forgive rather than punish. Of course, there are times when people and nations pushed God too far and were punished, but God ***prefers*** to forgive rather than punish because of his great kindness

God expresses his kindness towards sinners - we call it 'grace', treating us better than we deserve. God expresses his kindness towards sinners by being merciful, **not** treating us as we deserve to be treated. We see God's kindness embodied in Jesus Christ.

For example, when a woman caught in the act of adultery was brought before him, Jesus did not condone her sin, but he treated her kindly. Again, when a sinful woman came and anointed Jesus at a Pharisee's home, Jesus showed great kindness towards her. *'Your faith has saved you'* said Jesus. *'Go in peace'*

Think of Zacchaeus, think of the kindness shown to Simon Peter after his denial, think of any number of people in the gospel accounts. God's kindness was embodied in Jesus.

This is the amazing grace of God. Grace has its roots in God's character, in his kindness. But we have to say that God often has an ulterior motive. Really? you may say. Well, look at Romans 2:4 - *Do you show contempt for the riches of God's kindness, tolerance and patience, not realising that God's kindness leads you towards repentance?* God's ulterior motive with regard to sinners is that his kindness is designed to lead us to repentance.

But God also shows kindness towards believers, those already in a relationship with him. We wouldn't really expect otherwise, would we? In the Old Testament, the word used over and over again to describe God's kindness towards Israel is translated as 'loving-kindness' or 'covenant love', and God's kindness towards his people now includes followers of Christ. In this context, kindness, covenant love means also loyalty. God stands by his people.

The fruit of the Spirit is among other things kindness. And if the Holy Spirit dwells in us, and we are open to his working within us, and we allow the Holy Spirit to work within us, then surely we are going to find God's kindness coming and washing away all severity, any harshness, so that our behaviour towards others echoes God's attitude towards us, shown in Christ.

But, of course, we can resist. We can grieve the Holy Spirit by resisting all that he aims to do in our lives.

For example, some people have such a passion for righteousness that there seems to be little or no room left for compassion and kindness, and consequently the way they treat other people is nothing like the way Jesus treated people.

It's very easy to be hard and insensitive, unsympathetic and unkind towards those whom we deem to be failures in life, 'problem people', but how would Jesus have responded to 'problem people'? That's what we need to ask ourselves. I am sure the answer is that Jesus would have treated them with kindness rather than prejudice. How would Jesus have treated those whom we find embarrassing? With kindness. How would Jesus have treated those who always seem to be making demands on us, who we sometimes refer to as 'high maintenance' people?. With kindness. Have you ever noticed that the only time we ever see Jesus appearing to be unkind was when he came up against hypocrisy!

The Holy Spirit is working in us to enable us to treat people with the same kindness and consideration we see in Jesus, despite our efforts at times to hinder him. You see, as I said earlier, we all have this power to destroy people or to build them up. This is true no matter what our circumstances, no matter what our station in life.

Some of us manage to go through life completely untouched by the needs of those around us; sometimes we can be very selfish and not even realise it. Others see needs but just can't be bothered to act to address those needs. It's too much trouble, or it might interfere with their own plans. But there are others in whom God's Spirit is working, creating Christ-like kindness, and what confuses us is that these people are not always those whom we would identify as Christians!

The Holy Spirit sometimes exercises God's sovereign will and freedom by creating Christ-like graces in those who may not even profess faith in God, let alone in Jesus Christ!

This may confuse us, but it shouldn't cause too much concern, other than shaming us. Our concern should be that the Holy Spirit is freely able to create those Christ-like graces in us. ***love, joy, peace, patience and kindness*** and so on.

One thing I can guarantee. This coming week will be full of opportunities to show some kindness to other people, opportunities to exercise this tremendous power God has entrusted to us, opportunities to build people up in some way through an act or word of kindness. There are hundreds if not thousands of ways in which kindness can be expressed, but it'll cost us something in terms of our time, convenience, effort, money even.
For example -
- visiting the sick, elderly, lonely
- encouraging the discouraged or downhearted
- doing someone a favour without expecting anything at all in return
- running an errand
- sharing or even bearing a burden
- sharing joys and sorrows
- giving to the needy
- befriending the friendless
- phoning someone to ask how they are – something even the housebound themselves can do
- praying with someone
- offering a lift to church or to a meeting

The list of opportunities to *'brighten and cheer'* the lives of others is endless. May we be open to God's Spirit working in us to give us a new nature, helping us to watch out for and recognise and make the most of those opportunities.

Chapter Seven

The fruit of the Spirit is... goodness

In this chapter we are going to be considering moral philosophy or the question of ethical absolutes. "Goodness!" may well be your response. "Precisely!" is mine. Because we do indeed come to the sixth in this list that goes by the name of the Fruit of the Spirit – 'Goodness'!

The idea of goodness is a very flexible concept in the English language. The words 'good' and 'goodness' can be used in a variety of ways. For example, when I hear the word 'goodness' what do I think of? Sunday lunchtime when I was a child. Roast beef, Yorkshire pudding, potatoes and two other vegetables. And suddenly a young voice calls out, 'Mum, what are these lumps in the gravy? ***That's the goodness in it!***

Or I might recall an episode of Hancock's Half-Hour - 'Sunday Afternoon at Home' – where Tony Hancock is complaining about the gravy. 'I thought my mother was a bad cook,' he says. 'but at least her gravy used to move about!' 'That's the goodness in it!' says Hattie Jacques, defending her cooking skills, to which Hancock replies 'That's the half a pound of flour you put in it!'

Well, that's one use of the word 'goodness', but I suspect this is not what Paul had in mind!

'Goodness' can, of course, be understood in other ways too. We may talk about having a good time, for example, or if we are feeling unwell, we may say that we're not feeling too good today. Or it can be used disparagingly with the term 'do-gooder', which implies that people would rather commend a 'do-badder'!

In the New Testament we have the Good Samaritan, and the good news. And so we can see that this word and its associates can be used in various ways.

AA Milne once wrote a poem called ***The Good Little Girl.***

*It's funny how often they say to me, 'Jane? Have you been a **good** girl?'*

The little girl, Jane, is complaining that no matter where she's been, her parents always ask if she's been good, whether it was to the zoo or whatever. The last verse of the poem says:-

Well, what did they think that I went there to do?
and why should I want to be bad at the Zoo?
and should I be likely to say if I had?
So that's why it's funny of Mummy and Dad,
This asking and asking, in case I was bad,
'Well? Have you been a good girl, Jane?'

Of course, all this raises the question - *Who decides what's good or bad?* Whether it's gravy, or children's behaviour, or government policy or what, *who decides what's good or bad?*

There's no denying that there have been changes in morality, especially in recent years. I heard an interesting programme on Radio 4 some years ago, concerning Jesse Boot, the Nottingham man who started Boots The Chemists. Reference was made to the fact that until about 20 or 30 or so years ago, Boots would never stock or display contraceptives for fear of offending the morals of some of its customers, yet now they are on open display in Boots and many other places.

Do you remember Boots Lending Libraries? They had them in some cities and larger towns. Boots Lending Libraries never had books of a 'dubious nature' and yet such books are now openly on sale.

I was watching the film, 'Some Like It Hot' recently and at one point Jack Lemmon's character is having to impersonate a female in order to escape from a gangster mob. This leads to him getting engaged to a millionaire (male) and Tony Curtis's character says that you can't marry a man. It isn't allowed! Well, it is now!

Films that were banned from cinemas 30 or so years ago suddenly appear on our TV screens with hardly a murmur of protest.

Living together before or instead of marriage is accepted now as the norm, yet I remember the shock and scandal in the neighbourhood where I grew up when a couple across the road was discovered to be living together and not married.

Society's moral compass, its sense of right and wrong, good and bad, has changed, but how do we know if this itself is a good thing, or a bad thing? Who decides what is good or bad?

Some would say it's up to the freedom of the individual. Some will adopt the moral philosophy of the singer Sheryl Crow *'If it makes you happy - how can it be bad?'*

Freedom of expression, individual freedom, the 'feel-good factor' - these are the ways some people judge what's good and what's bad. Others would say the majority view determines what's right and wrong. Some moral choices are determined on the basis of 'the greatest good for the greatest number of people'. This is the way governments often have to make decisions.

Some would say that love is the standard for goodness. This is the approach of 'situation ethics'. It invites us to ask the question - *what is the most loving thing to do in a particular situation?* Sounds attractive, doesn't it? Suppose a Christian mother of, say, 3 or 4 children is living in a country where Christians are persecuted. Her husband has already been shot so she is the sole provider and carer for her children. Suppose she is arrested, leaving behind her family to fend for themselves.

Imagine that she is guaranteed her release on condition that she totally renounces her faith and is prepared to utter vile obscenities about Jesus Christ. The *loving* thing to do would be to think of her family and fulfil the condition with her lips at least. That's what situation ethics would say, but would that be right or wrong? It would make an interesting discussion topic, wouldn't it?

Who decides what's good or bad? And on what basis?

There are even those who would say that there is no such thing as morality. Behaviour is determined by a person's environment, upbringing, and some even say, by chemical reactions and electrical impulses in the brain, which has the appeal of suggesting we are not responsible or accountable for our behaviour.

Such views, however, are not the scriptural view.

Faced then with the question *what is goodness*? we could spend a great deal of time looking at the details of the various 'isms' of moral philosophy - relativism, determinism, behaviourism, situationism - but as Christians we look in a different direction to discover what is right and wrong, what is good or evil.

The Bible plainly teaches us that **God is good.**
Psalm 25 *__Good__ and upright is the Lord,*
Psalm 100 *Enter his gates with thanksgiving and his courts with praise; give thanks to him and praise his name. for the Lord is __good__ and his love endures for ever.*
Nahum 1:7 *The Lord is __good__, a refuge in times of trouble - he cares for those who trust in him.*
In Matthew 19 Jesus himself said that only God is good.

The Bible also speaks of the good works of God, the good gifts of God, the good Word of God, God's good pleasure, God's good and perfect will.

God is **good**! and only God is truly good. And he

determines what is right and wrong, not the majority, not the individual, not those electrical impulses in our brain cells, not our feelings and emotions.

Whatever God does is good. This may confuse us sometimes because there are many things we don't understand, many things we would do differently if we were God, or so we think, but then we have to recognise that human love, human knowledge, human wisdom, our grasp of truth, our understanding of situations are all incomplete and imperfect, whereas God is holy and pure, his love is perfect, his knowledge is complete. Faith is about living without the answers to many of our questions, and trusting God's perfect goodness.

Whatever God does is good because God is good, and his goodness is the standard.

Goodness then is, in the first place, about pleasing God and expressing something of the divine character in our lives.

What does this mean? Firstly it means **knowing** what is good. And this means being open to all that God has revealed concerning his character, his will, his purposes and values.

In one of the earlier chapters of this book I wrote that the Holy Spirit wants us to put roots down deep into the word of God. Psalm 1:3 says *(the righteous person's) delight is in the law of the Lord (i.e. word of God) and on his law he meditates day and night. He is like a tree planted by streams of water, which yields its fruit in season and whose leaf does not wither.*

The Word of God, the Scriptures, are the most reliable revelation of the mind of God, the character of God, the will and purposes of God, the *goodness* of God, and the Holy Spirit is able to re-create this fruit in our lives as we read, mark and inwardly digest the Word of God.

Goodness is about knowing God's Word and ***obeying*** God's Word. It's no use just studying the Bible as an academic exercise. It is no good meditating day and night if we never take the vital step of putting into practice what we discover. It is no good just filling brain cells with memory verses if that's all they are, memory verses. The Holy Spirit can only reproduce goodness in our lives if we are willing to obey.

But even then, when we've said this, we haven't said everything about goodness. Jesus made it very clear that goodness is much more than outward conformity to the Law. Matthew 5:20 ***I tell you that unless your righteousness <u>surpasses</u> that of the Pharisees and the teachers of the law, you will certainly not enter the Kingdom of Heaven.*** The Scribes and Pharisees saw goodness as consisting of obedience to the law of God, - keeping the commandments, outward obedience, maintaining the appearance of righteousness, but Jesus taught that it involves more than this. Goodness includes our motives, our thoughts. Goodness begins <u>within</u> us.

Jesus said that good actions could no more proceed from a person harbouring evil thoughts than good fruit from a rotten, diseased tree. Goodness is about character as well as conduct. It isn't simply a matter of adding up good deeds and setting them against evil deeds, and making sure we stay in credit. That was how the Scribes and Pharisees saw it - an excess of good deeds over evil ones. But goodness is about character as well as conduct.

Billy Graham writes ***A good heart, like a good spring, perpetually pours out goodness.***

So goodness is not just about doing good, although it should include this. As Matthew Henry puts it: *Being ready to do good to all, as we have opportunity.* But goodness begins deep within; it describes character and that's why it is part of the Fruit of the Spirit.

Isaiah 64:6 sums up our real situation: ***all <u>our</u> righteous*** *acts are like filthy rags*. There is no way that we can manufacture a righteousness, holiness, goodness that will satisfy God, or even satisfy ourselves. Remember what Paul said in Romans 7? *I have the desire to do good, but I cannot carry it out... What I want to do I do not do, but what I hate I do.*

And even if we manage to achieve some semblance of goodness, doing good deeds, and even teaching others how to be good and obedient, the Bible says it won't last. *Your goodness is like the morning mist; like the early dew that disappears.* (Hosea 6:4).

True goodness comes through the activity of the Holy Spirit and we can never succeed in creating it by our own efforts. We depend utterly and completely on God's Holy Spirit for genuine goodness, which means we need to begin each day praying words of David in Psalm 51 - *Create in me a pure heart, O God, and renew a right spirit within me. Do not cast me from your presence; or take your Holy Spirit from me.* We need to ask the Holy Spirit to guard us from adopting the shifting morality of the age. We need to study scriptures so that God's Spirit can teach us what is good and so that our concept of right and wrong is shaped by the Word of God and not newspapers and TV.

Rom 12:2 *Do not conform any longer to the pattern of this world, but be transformed by the renewing of your mind. Then you will be able to test and approve what God's will is - his GOOD, pleasing and perfect will*

The scriptures teach us that goodness consists of *whatever is true, whatever is noble, whatever is right, whatever is pure, whatever is lovely, whatever is admirable* (Philippians 4:8)

May God grant us the knowledge of what is good and pleasing to him and is in accordance with his perfect will.
May the Spirit of God so work in us that love, joy, peace,

patience, kindness and goodness become so characteristic of our lives that we remind others of Christ Jesus - *who died to make us **good.***

Chapter Eight

The fruit of the Spirit is… faithfulness

Faithfulness is an idea most of us are familiar with. Those couples who choose to marry in a church promise to be faithful. The words used in the introduction at the beginning of the Wedding Service are something like this: *Marriage is given so that husband and wife may comfort and help each other, living faithfully together, in need and in plenty, in sorrow and in joy.* And then the bride and groom each promise lifelong faithfulness to one another.

Church members, at some point ,will have made a promise (or at least implied a promise) to be faithful. Certainly when I have welcomed people into membership in churches where I was the minister I will have asked the person to promise that they will be a *loyal member of (whatever the name of the church is), regular in attending worship, and **faithful** in your support for the church'*

What does it mean, 'faithfulness'? To be faithful is to be accurate, to be true to fact, to be true to our word, to be loyal, trustworthy, reliable, conscientious, responsible. Faithfulness is *that which makes a person one on whom others can depend.*

As always we have to remember that in the context of the 'fruit of the Spirit' *faithfulness* is an aspect of God's character that the Holy Spirit is aiming to reproduce in every Christian believer. The *faithfulness* Paul has in mind there in Galatians 5 is seen first and foremost in God himself.

What can we say concerning God's **faithfulness**?

1. God's faithfulness means **commitment.**

Almighty God, the creator, the ruler of universe, the

mighty and powerful God, the fount of all truth, knowledge and wisdom, holiness and purity, the King of Kings and Lord of Lords is a God who is a committed God, committed above all else, it seems, to the human race, to you and to me. At least, that is the way God has revealed himself to us.

Ever since God created the first human beings, whether it was millions of years ago or just over 6000 years ago, his commitment to the human race has been without question. God's commitment never wavered even when it meant Adam and Eve had to be ejected from the Garden of Eden.

What happened after they had been banished? Genesis 4 tells us that *Adam lay with his wife Eve, and she became pregnant and gave birth to Cain. She said, 'With the help of the LORD I have brought forth a man.'* Eve didn't seem to think that God had stayed behind in the Garden of Eden, did she? And she was right. God was still with Adam and Eve, and as the story unfolds, it's quite clear that God had indeed stayed with them and continued to journey with his people.

God's commitment never wavered, even when God's special people, those whom he had chosen to be channels of grace, points of light in a dark world, even when God's chosen people were unfaithful and disobedient.

God remained committed until, in the fulness of time, God became man and walked the earth in human form. Jesus Christ is the tangible expression, the physical embodiment of God's commitment to us. And this commitment still continues and is seen in the history of the world and of the Church. It's seen in the guarding and the handing on of the gospel message from one generation to the next down through the centuries, and we rejoice in the assurance that God is still faithful, still committed to our world, and to each of us as individuals.

2. God's faithfulness is **active.**

You don't hear much these days of Gordon Bailey but Gordon Bailey was an evangelist back in the late 1960s/70s. He wasn't the usual kind of evangelist, but Gordon Bailey broke new ground in his way of communicating. He had first trained as a clown, and it is not surprising therefore that he used a great deal of humour in presenting the gospel message. Gordon Bailey used to appear on the late night epilogue on Midlands TV and on one occasion he dressed as a dirty tramp, looking as if he hadn't washed for weeks. He began to declare his belief in soap, his faith in soap and how important soap was to him. He spoke of his commitment to the whole concept, the whole idea of soap, but it was quite apparent that it was not an active commitment.

On another occasion he dressed as a mountaineer, with all the equipment, ropes and chains, hefty boots, hooks and a hammer and whatever else a mountaineer uses. This time he spoke at length about mountaineering, using all the right words, jargon, terminology. He described the techniques of rock-climbing, and was in full flow until someone asked him if he had ever been mountaineering. 'Well, no! not exactly!' he replied. Again his commitment wasn't an active commitment.

Faithfulness and commitment must be seen in action. We see throughout the Old Testament in God's dealings with Abraham, Isaac, Jacob, Joseph the dreamer, Moses, the Hebrew slaves whom God liberated from slavery and led through the wilderness for forty years. We see God's faithfulness in action with the wayward people of God during the times of the prophets who themselves, together with their messages were signs of God's faithfulness in action.

Supremely, of course, God's faithfulness in action was expressed so wonderfully in the birth of Jesus Christ, and in his life, teachings, healings, befriending of people, his compassion and his love expressed in so many ways. Ultimately we see God's faithfulness demonstrated when Christ surrendered his life for our sakes.

On Easter Day we celebrate God's faithfulness in action, when he raised Jesus from the dead.

3. God's faithfulness is **risky.**

Ever since early times dogs have been recognised for their faithfulness. Fido is a traditional name for a dog, which looks remarkably like the Latin verb meaning to trust or rely on. Early tombs would sometimes have a dog carved out and lying at the feet of a married woman as a symbol of faithfulness and protectiveness. The stone memorial at Beddgelert in North Wales tells the story of Prince Llewellyn's dog, Gelert, and how on one occasion Llewellyn went hunting without his dog, leaving Gelert to guard Llewellyn's infant son at the hunting lodge. Llewellyn returned from the hunt to be greeted by his dog but the Prince was alarmed to see blood stains on the dog. And then he saw the baby's cradle overturned, and Llewellyn suspected the worst and killed his dog. He had acted in haste but repented at leisure when he turned the cradle over and found his son alive and well. Gelert had defended the baby during an attack by wolves.

It's a nice story! Pity though that it is just a story started by an enterprising 18th century innkeeper! The village is actually named after St Kelert's grave! But the story reminds us that faithfulness is risky, and God's faithfulness includes the willingness to take risks. The risk of failure, defeat, rejection.

Christ's faithfulness was clearly seen to be risky. He was despised and rejected by men (as Isaiah puts it), a man of sorrows and familiar with suffering. Faithfulness took Jesus all the way to the cross and death and that awful, terrible moment when it seemed as if he was utterly alone, abandoned even by his Father.

4. God's faithfulness is about **perseverance**, which is another word for that unwavering commitment,

persevering against all odds, against all obstacles, against all human reason (we might say), and pressing on towards the objective, the goal.

5. God's faithfulness requires **faith.** In this context, this means a belief that the aim is worthwhile, that we – you and I – are worth saving. The Holy Spirit aims to change us and remake us in the image of Christ, to enable us to become like Christ, and God's faithfulness affirms that he believes this to be worthwhile.

How does all this translate in terms of our faithfulness?

1. What about our **commitment**? Commitment to God and his will and purposes, to the church, to one another, to worship and service, even commitment to ourselves and to being the best that we can be, reaching our full potential in Christ. Commitment is about **responsible discipleship**, yet what is lacking so often in today's church, and, indeed, today's society? Commitment!

I am convinced that the Christian Church in this country is operating on less than half-power for two reasons:

(a) we are content to plod on with little or no interference from the Holy Spirit, and
(b) as individuals, so many of us lack the commitment seen in the Early Church, and seen also in many other parts of the world, in what are usually called deprived or developing countries.

Faithfulness and commitment mean accepting our God-given responsibilities and duties as Christians.

2. How **active** is our commitment, which for us means obedience, just as it did for Christ: ***he humbled himself and became <u>obedient</u> to death – even death on a cross!*** (Philippians 2)

In industry and commerce there's an expression 'turn around time'. It refers to the time taken between placing an order and delivery. Public services and other companies all have their target 'turn around times'. For example, how long it takes from reporting a fault to having the fault investigated and put right.

The Green Flag car breakdown service promises a 'turn around time' of one hour and if they haven't responded to the call out within one hour, they compensate the motorist with £10. I don't know whether it's good or bad that they very often arrive after about 55 minutes!

In terms of God's commands, God's call, what's your 'turn around time'? How long is the delay between the order and delivery or a positive response?

God began calling me into ordained ministry as long ago as 1973. I answered that call in 1980 when I went to theological college. A seven year turn around time, 10 or 11 years in terms of actually becoming an ordained minister. Not a very good 'turn around time'!

My 'turn around time' for baptism was probably about half that time but it was still nothing to be proud of!

What about you? Perhaps God is calling you to service in the church or in the community. There are always opportunities for volunteers. Or it may be something else that God is prompting you to do. Some simple act of kindness, for example, or peace-making, repairing a broken relationship, or the challenge to make more time for God each day. Faithfulness is about obedience, a short 'turn around time'.

3. Faithfulness is **risky**, of course. For most of us, the biggest risk is that it may interfere with our lifestyle, comfort, priorities, but it can be riskier than that, of course.

In my teens I would often organise rambles for our church, usually in the Peak District. Sometimes these included walks near Eyam, known by many as the village hit by the Great Plague in the 17th century. The Rector of Eyam was William Mompesson. He was responsible for acting quickly to isolate the village from adjacent villages, not to protect his own villagers but to prevent the disease from spreading further. He sent his own children away to some safe place and wanted his wife to go also while he remained. She was faithful and refused to go. This in itself was risky and her decision cost her her life. Something like two-thirds of the population of Eyam died.

Clearly Mompesson's own faithfulness put him at risk also as he served his parishioners in the name of Christ, and as he encouraged them to remain within the village boundaries to prevent the plague spreading to other villages.

We could offer countless other examples of the risk of being faithful to our calling, our commitment to the commands of Christ and the demands of Christian love.

4. Faithfulness involves **perseverance.**

Back in the 1992 Olympic Games the athlete Derek Redmond gave a gift to preachers, without even realising it. You may recall that Derek Redmond pulled a muscle when he was on the back straight of the track. It looked like a hamstring injury. Redmond was writhing in agony on the ground. The race finished and he was still there. Then suddenly he stood up and started hobbling round the track, staying in his lane, determined to finish the race.

He came round the last bend, clearly in terrible pain. From personal experience I would say that, if he had walked backwards, he would have found it less painful, but he persevered.

Then what happened? His father came on to the track, brushing aside anyone trying to stop him. He comforted his son and supported him for the rest of the distance.

What a picture of a father's love and faithfulness and commitment! But then what happened? An official came on to the track, trying to deter Redmond from completing his race, trying to put him off, but the father waved him away, and continued to support his son all the way! Faithfulness and perseverance!

Just as an aside, the crowd of spectators cheered him all the way to the finishing line, which always reminds me of Hebrews 12 *Therefore, since we are surrounded by such a great cloud of witnesses, let us throw off everything that hinders and the sin that so easily entangles. And let us run with perseverance the race marked out for us, fixing our eyes on Jesus, the pioneer and perfecter of our faith.*

Our faithfulness may be sorely, painfully tested and challenged, and we may be tempted to give up, or we may find ourselves distracted by materialism, by this world's trinkets designed to divert us, but, as Paul says *Forgetting what is behind and straining towards what is ahead, I press on towards the goal to win the prize for which God has called me heavenwards in Christ Jesus*

There were no medals for Derek Redmond, but he had the satisfaction of finishing the race. He finished what he set out to do. We are promised, not a medal but a *crown of life* if we persevere. *Be faithful, even to the point of death and I will give you the crown of life.*

5. Faithfulness requires **faith**, believing that it's all worthwhile, that becoming like Christ is worth all the struggle and the waiting. It may be a long slow process because we will not necessarily loosen our grip overnight on the habits and the attitudes of a lifetime, but we need to believe that it's worth all the struggle and the waiting.

Faithfulness also requires faith in God, trust in God, belief in his good purposes and his faithfulness, belief in his love and in his saving power

Faithfulness also requires faith in the Scriptures, where we find God's will and purposes and promises revealed.

It requires faith in the power of prayer, maintaining contact and fellowship with our heavenly Father, drawing on his strength and help and grace.

One day we shall stand before Christ to give an account of our lives, and we'll be judged, not according to how successful been in the eyes of the world, but how faithful we have been in God's sight and in the place where he has put us. Our salvation will not depend on this judgement and its outcome; our sins that separate us from God have been decisively dealt with on the cross. But we still have to give an account and the Bible does suggest that rewards are involved in the outcome.

The Apostle Paul was by no means perfect, but if he had been able to write his own epitaph it would have been **I have kept the faith.** He had been faithful and he knew this to be the work of the Holy Spirit.

May we too be worthy of the same epitaph: **I have kept the faith** because we have allowed the Holy Spirit to work in us and have responded to his prompting.

Chapter Nine

The fruit of the Spirit is… gentleness

When the Holy Spirit creates the fruit of the Spirit in our lives, what is he doing? He is bringing alive God's image, God's character in our lives, which means that God is loving, joyful, patient, kind, good, faithful and ***gentle.***

We have a touring caravan which, of course, we take on holiday. We haven't always been caravanners. There was a time when our holiday home was a tent, originally a large ridge tent when there were just three of us, my wife, myself and our son. Then we progressed till eventually we had a 6 berth tent for ourselves and our four children.

I recall some years ago we had a holiday near Pembroke. We had a friend who was the Rector in one of the villages. The rectory had a large walled garden with plenty of space for our tent as well as several vegetable beds, not to mention two or three peacocks that used to wander into the garden. Our friend, David, was chaplain to the local lifeboat, and he came to us one evening to warn us that they were expecting a force 9 storm that night, and *'would you rather come inside and stay in the Rectory tonight?'*

I thanked him and said it was tempting but I would rather stay with the tent to make sure it was still there the next morning. True enough, a storm blew up, and I can tell you that gentleness is not the most obvious characteristic of God when you're lying under canvas at three o'clock in the morning, with tent poles creaking and the tent flapping, and this force 9 wind howling around you, even in the comparative shelter of the walled garden.

We have had similar experiences at other times, even in the caravan when a sudden gust feels like it's going to move the caravan to a slightly different position a few inches away. The first year we went to France we experienced a violent storm that came upon us with little or no warning! It took our awning and flung it over the top of the caravan.

Gentleness is not the most obvious characteristic of God when winds are hitting your temporary holiday home at 60 mph, or more, and when it feels like your fragile world is about to crash down upon you.

Of course, there are times when people's homes – often more substantial than our tent or caravan - do fall down upon them as hurricanes and tornadoes rip through towns and cities and villages. It isn't easy to think of God's gentleness when we hear of earthquakes, cyclones, tidal waves, floods, volcanoes.

God is revealed in his creation but what do we see? Not always gentleness but awesome power at times. And when we then focus in, as Tennyson puts it, on *nature, red in tooth and claw,* we still find it hard to see the gentleness of God.

But isn't it true that even in the created world around us there are signs, hints of God's gentleness? For example, a butterfly, so light and seemingly fragile, the delicate petals of a flower, the feathers of a bird, seed parachutes of dandelions, and we could find many other examples of the gentler side of creation.

God's gentleness, however, is seen most clearly not in what is called **general** revelation but in **special** revelation, in the coming into this world of his Son Jesus Christ.

Jesus said: ***He who has seen me has seen the Father.*** If we want to know what God is like, there are hints, clues in creation but, says Jesus *look at me! listen to me!*

What do we see and hear? Matthew 11:29 ***Take my yoke upon you and learn from me, for I am gentle and***

humble in heart.

We see Jesus who took little children, considered at that time to be of little or no value, and he welcomed them and showed us children have a very special place in the heart of God; he showed gentleness towards children.

In Christ's dealings with broken people, those who had been unable to keep to the strict demands of the Law, sinners and outcasts, we see gentleness. Jesus never condoned the sin but he showed gentleness towards the sinner.

Jesus gave dignity, value, to women, treating them always with respect and gentleness.

His healing ministry was not seen in the frantic ritual we sometimes witness in the healing 'circuses' that travel around our country from time to time, but Christ was always sensitive and gentle. He confirmed the words of the Psalmist...
The Lord is compassionate and gracious, slow to anger, abounding in love... he does not treat us as our sins deserve or repay us according to our iniquities... as a father has compassion on his children, so the Lord has compassion on those who fear him; for he knows how we are formed, he remembers that we are dust...

Don't these words speak to us of gentleness? God's gentleness.

What then does gentleness mean?

William Barclay tells us that the Greek word, *praotes,* is the *'most untranslatable of words'* but then Barclay says that of quite a few Greek words!

Aristotle said that this word *describes the person who is so much in control of himself that he is always angry at the right time, and never angry at the wrong time.*

Matthew Henry says : *A gentle person is one who is not easily provoked, and if he is, he is soon pacified.* Gentleness is *a disposition that is even-tempered, tranquil, balanced in spirit, unpretentious, and that has the passions under control.*

This Greek word is sometimes translated 'meekness', but more often than not it seems to be related to anger. A gentle spirit is the opposite of an angry spirit. Gentleness is about self-control in relation to anger, it's about a quiet strength and confidence.

In Isaiah's *servant* passages we find a description of this quiet strength, this gentleness, in the face of all kinds of provocation:

Isaiah 42:1-3a '**Here is my servant, whom I uphold, my chosen one in whom I delight; I will put my Spirit on him and he will bring justice to the nations. He will not shout or cry out, or raise his voice in the streets. A bruised reed he will not break, and a smouldering wick he will not snuff out.**

Isaiah 53 **He was oppressed and afflicted, yet he did not open his mouth; he was led like a lamb to the slaughter, and as a sheep before her shearers is silent, so he did not open his mouth.**

This Servant described by Isaiah is clearly identified in the New Testament as being Jesus Christ, the creator of the universe who became a servant for our sakes. Jesus was knocked about, ridiculed, abused, spat upon, and yet he showed no anger, no desire for retaliation. Christ could have summoned multitudes of angels to rescue him from the cross, but he didn't.

So, if we want to know what gentleness is, it is power, strength, anger under control as seen in Jesus Christ.

But when we see not a glimmer, not a spark of retaliation or revenge, no demands for justice and rights, no claims of privilege, we have to say such gentleness is not natural. After all, from our youngest days we have been brought up to stand up for ourselves. As the parents of four children, more than once we've come up against bullying and, like most parents, we have had to tell our children to stand up for themselves. It isn't natural to advocate that we should allow the playground bully to walk all over us. It isn't natural to come under severe provocation, to be wrongly accused, or misrepresented, or attacked (verbally or otherwise), or unfairly criticised, and not be tempted to hit back. Gentleness, meekness, submissiveness do not come naturally, but only through the ministry of the Holy Spirit.

What does all this mean in practice then? Gentleness finds expression on two fronts' Firstly, towards one another. Over and over again Paul piles up words of exhortation to members of the early church, urging them to be gentle towards one another. In Colossians he says ***you must rid yourselves of... anger, rage, malice, slander... clothe yourselves with compassion, kindness, humility, gentleness and patience.*** In Philippians 4... ***Let your gentleness be evident to all***. In Ephesians 4... ***get rid of all bitterness, rage and anger, brawling and slander along with every form of malice.*** Get rid of all this and what do we have? Gentleness. Gentleness should be the hallmark of our dealings with one another in the family of God, and where it's absent it's a sure sign that the Holy Spirit is struggling to break through into hard, resistant hearts.

What does this mean in practice? It means when our feathers are ruffled by someone, we should not rise up defensively.

A Christian lady once went to see her pastor to tell him what she had to put up with at home. The pastor had the courage to confront her with the fact of her angry, bitter spirit, and she rose to her own defence. *You'd be angry if you lived with a man who treated you like dirt and walked all over you!*

In no way did the pastor condone the way the man was treating his wife especially as this husband was a Christian too, but he dared to suggest to the woman that she had two problems. She was surprised and said *Did I hear you correctly? Two problems? I only have one - my husband!*

The pastor said - *Two problems. Your husband is one, but your attitude towards your husband is another. Until you face up to this and look to God for a proper attitude, even in these circumstances, you will grieve the Holy Spirit and continue to have not one but two problems.*

Fortunately the woman accepted her pastor's word and underwent an amazing transformation. She treasured her relationship with Christ so much above all else, and she claimed the Scripture promise that God would **supply all her needs according to his riches in glory through Christ Jesus,** and she began to experience victory over anger and bitterness and all those emotions and attitudes which are the opposite of gentleness

Her testimony was that instead of waiting for a change in her husband's behaviour, she literally changed his behaviour by hers. No wonder the Holy Spirit seeks to create and cultivate gentleness in us, for gentleness has the power to change others.

Gentleness is, of course, a relationship word, but Archbishop Trench says: *Gentleness is not just about a man's outward behaviour, nor just about his relationships with his fellowmen. Rather it is an inwrought grace of the soul, and the exercises of it are chiefly towards God.*

Gentleness towards God? I have to confess that when I'm lying there in my tent in the early hours of the morning , or even looking out of the caravan window at another rainy day when on holiday, I don't always feel gentle towards God! I suspect I may not be alone in that.

It doesn't seem fair, until I begin to think of the plight of so many people in the world for whom a holiday would come very low on their list of priorities. At least we have food, shelter, peace and security and even if the tent canvas is torn to shreds, or the caravan is blown over in gales, it isn't the end of the world. It isn't usually life-threatening. It might be a bit alarming but it is not usually life threatening!

I know that on many occasions, on sleepless nights with rain pounding on the roof of the tent, God has gently turned my anxiety and fear into prayer for others.

Jesus himself was, of course, the supreme example of this gentleness, gentle submissiveness to the divine will. He spent something like 18 years engaged in in the commonplace drudgery of a carpenter's workshop, and then left the security of home to go and face crowds of people in order to deliver God's message. Why? In submission to the will of God.

On the cross not only did he show gentleness towards his fellow humans who nailed him to the cross, but not once did Christ complain that it was unfair, and 'why should this happen to him?' and 'what had he done to deserve such treatment?'

Jesus himself is an example of divine gentleness and the Holy Spirit is seeking to reproduce this gentleness in you and me.

So what are you going to do? Cling to the fact that such gentleness is unnatural, that we can't help the way we are. Or will you allow the Holy Spirit to come and change you and re-make you in the likeness of Christ?

Chapter Ten

The fruit of the Spirit is… self-control

The last of these nine Christian virtues is **self-control** and I want to explore this topic in this chapter with reference to Paul's Letter to Titus, for there we find the expression, or associated ideas used repeatedly in Titus 2, although it must be acknowledged that the Greek word used in Titus 2 is not the same as that used by Paul in Galatians 5.

First a bit of background. Paul's letter to Titus was written as a pastoral letter, written to help Titus in his leadership role in the church on Crete. It was written to advise this young leader as to how he should instruct and lead the people there.

Titus was Greek and was probably converted through Paul's preaching, which is why Paul refers to him as '*my true son in our common faith*'

Paul had left Titus there on the island of Crete, in his words in 1:5, *that you might straighten out what was left unfinished, and appoint elders in every town as I directed you.* Or as we find it in the New King James Version, *that you should set in order the things that are lacking.*

Well, if it was a matter of what was lacking in Crete, we might well say "not a lot" on the face of it. The Cretans lived life to the full in worldly terms. Theirs was a society dedicated to acquiring wealth, and fulfilling whatever lust or desire you might have. It was a society where integrity and honesty meant very little, and where morality took a back seat and wealth and material gain, even by dishonest means, were in the driving seat.

It is all summed up in 1:12 - *Even one of their own prophets has said: 'Cretans are always liars, evil brutes, lazy gluttons.'*

So in worldly terms not much was lacking, but in terms of morality and in spiritual terms they were paupers.

In 1:10-14, we also see that there were people – influential people, presumably – who were directly opposed to sound doctrine and who were *teaching things that ought not to be taught – and that for dishonest gain.*

This, then is the context of this letter to Titus. How then was Titus going to set about sorting these problems out and dealing with these false teachers? The answer is by setting an example of what a faithful follower of Christ looks like, and by teaching the Christians in Crete what it means to live godly lives, based on scripture and sound doctrine.

In these verses in chapter 2 Paul shows what this meant in practice for various categories of people in the church.

First of all the older men. This does not refer to the "elders" who bore office in the church, since they had already been dealt with in chapter 1. These words are for **all** the older men in the congregation!

The Cretans were *liars, evil brutes, lazy gluttons.* The older Christian men must therefore be distinctive by being *temperate, worthy of respect.*

Note that - <u>worthy</u> of respect, rather than demanding it or expecting it by virtue of their seniority.

This means they should set an example by being *of good, honest character, self-controlled and sound in faith, love and in endurance.* I wonder how many of these we older men could tick off in a list?

And just in case the older women were feeling smug, Paul turns his attention to them... *teach the older women to be reverent,* respectful in the way they live, *– not*

***slanderers** (gossips – telling lies about people, or making things up to fill the gaps),* **or addicted to much wine** *(teach them to ease off on their drinking habits!) and in this way they'll be setting an example – a good example to the younger women, encouraging them* **to love their husbands and children, to be self-controlled and pure, to be busy at home, to be kind, and to be subject to their husbands, so that no one will malign the word of God.**

So in addressing the older women Paul addresses also the younger women, or at least shows Titus what his aim is for them too.

Notice this also in passing. Paul does not tell Titus what to teach the young women. He tells Titus what to teach the **older** women to teach the younger women. We have a glimpse there of Paul's wisdom. Titus was himself a fairly young man, so it was probably best to let the older women do the teaching, not least because their example would be far more powerful than Titus' words.

But I wonder how comfortable we are with these instructions. The younger women were *to love their husbands and children* (no problem there), *to be busy at home* (a raised eyebrow or two perhaps?) and *to be subject to their husbands.* Gasp! You can't say that sort of thing nowadays! Completely out of order! Such ideas would not go down too well these days. Indeed such teaching might provoke people to "malign the word of God" if we were to advocate this sort of thing nowadays.

To modern ears, this teaching probably conjures up a picture of overbearing tyrannical husbands and the little woman in her pinny, cowering behind her vacuum cleaner, or chained to the kitchen sink!

Understand this. Paul is not giving husbands permission to abuse, belittle or bully their wives.

By the way, the New Testament also says "***be subject to one another, submit to one another***" (Ephesians 5:21) but this doesn't seem to cause quite such a stir, probably because most of us disregard it anyway! Our 21st century culture says *submit to no one!*

What it actually means is <u>choosing</u> to take second place, deferring to the other person. So when Paul says in Ephesians 5 *"Wives submit to your husbands"* he does not mean become a 2nd class citizen, or that the wife is in any way inferior. It means choose to give your husband first place (after Christ) or choose to take second place. Notice what follows there in Ephesians. Paul says ***"Husbands love your wives"*** which in practice also means "give your wife first place (after Christ) and you yourselves take second place!". But before we move on, notice also ***Love your wives as Christ loved the church and gave himself up for it***. I take that to mean, *be prepared to die for your wife!*

The problem in Crete, and Ephesus, and other cities at that time was this. Early Christianity was so pro-female that some of the women got carried away and began causing disorder in their families and in the church. They were standing up in church making challenging statements, arguing with leaders and teachers, challenging their husbands, and just generally being belligerent and disruptive, so Paul encourages women to maintain order, to be respectable, and to use their newly-found freedom wisely and carefully. And in that society and culture (and dare I say today also), as long as the husband wasn't overbearing and cruel and unkind but "sound in faith and love", then an orderly household working well, working harmoniously, where people – both husband and wife - understood their responsibilities, would honour God's word and the gospel.

We appear to have wandered a long way away from the topic of 'self-control' but not if you think about it because this teaching isn't about being controlling, but **self**-controlling.

And in case they're feeling left out, there's a word about young men too. They too should be self-controlled, and in v 7 we see that this meant integrity, seriousness (although there is a place for a sense of humour and fun, but we need to know also when to be serious), and soundness of speech (i.e. know what you're talking about or keep quiet!)

As a young man himself, Titus was expected, encouraged to be a role model to the other young men by displaying these qualities. As the leader, Titus had a particular duty to be a good role model for every one, but Paul's instructions were really about **everyone**, especially older people, being good role models.

The Greek word translated in v 7 as "*example*" actually means *model* or *replica.* Replica of whom? Of Christ himself who was the perfect example, role model of how we should act.

I would suggest the over-arching word or expression here to describe Christ and all who follow him is indeed this expression, ***self-control***

What Paul is wanting Titus to teach the people here are various ways of being **self-controlled.**

Self-control - something we all have difficulty with in one way or another, whether it's showing restraint when we smell or see or even mention chocolate, or giving up smoking, or when we're shopping, or gossiping, or speaking sharp, harmful, unkind words, or even staying awake during long sermons! Or at least trying to keep sermons to a reasonable length! Self-control – living the kind of life and thinking and saying and doing the kind of things that are acceptable to God does not come easily for most of us.

In his book - **Rolling In The Aisles** - Murray Watts tells of a Methodist Minister who was very self-disciplined in every sphere of life except for one secret vice. He loved cherry brandy. Of course, he couldn't openly admit this to his congregation as they were old fashioned Methodists and therefore strictly teetotal.

Some mischievous friends knew about his secret and decided to exploit the situation for a bit of fun, so they offered him a whole crate of cherry brandy on one condition. He had to acknowledge the gift publicly in the next church magazine. The minister accepted the challenge, the magazine was duly published, and a note from the minister said this... *The Minister would like to thank his friends for the generous gift of fruit... ... and the spirit in which it was given.*

Self-control, self-discipline, self-restraint, call it what you will, does not come easily. What's the key to this struggle? Perhaps first of all it's this. In a sense *self-control* is perhaps a bit of a misnomer and misleading.

The Greek word means "power/mastery over self" which does not necessarily mean us having complete control over ourselves. Self-control isn't so much about **us** controlling ourselves but the control of self, and there is a subtle and important difference here. The "control of self" can include being controlled by someone other than ourselves, and if we're thinking about the fruit of the Holy Spirit, then that "someone" is surely the Holy Spirit influencing us and enabling us to get a grip on ourselves.

In terms of the fruit of the Spirit, **self-control** is the control of self by the Holy Spirit, and the aim is to create a life that can be a worthy offering to God.

William Barclay says *self-control is that quality of a person which makes him able to live and walk in the world yet remain pure and untainted* and it begins with the mind, the renewal of the mind by the Holy Spirit. Romans 12:2 ***Do not conform any longer to the pattern of this world but BE <u>transformed by the renewing of your mind</u>***

In the Sermon on the Mount, Jesus taught that self-control begins in the mind. ***You have heard that it was said "Do not commit adultery. But I tell you that anyone who looks at a woman lustfully has already committed adultery with her in his heart***

The battle for self-control begins, and dare I say, ends in the mind. Often we simply can't help the thoughts that pop into our heads, although we need to realise that sometimes we can! We can so easily fill our heads with all kinds of rubbish, all the images and words we absorb (not least through our televisions). No wonder then that sometimes impure thoughts and all kinds of unwholesome attitudes creep in! But often we can't help the thoughts that pop into our heads, but we **can** influence whether or not they remain there, and self-control is about allowing the Holy Spirit to bring discipline to our thinking.

Perhaps the Holy Spirit works by bringing to mind some scripture such as Phil 4:8 - ***whatever is true, whatever is noble, whatever is right, whatever is pure, whatever is lovely, whatever is admirable—if anything is excellent or praiseworthy—think about such things.*** although the Holy Spirit won't bring such verses to mind if we haven't read them and memorised them!

So the control of self begins with the mind and it touches upon so many aspects of life, and all the time the Holy Spirit is aiming to create a life worthy of being offered to God.

Self-control is an important aspect of Christian discipleship. It isn't an optional extra but a fundamental part, and yet no amount of self-effort will ever create it. For this and all the virtues described as the fruit of the Spirit we need the help of the Holy Spirit. ***The fruit of the Spirit is love, joy, peace, patience, kindness, goodness, faithfulness, gentleness and self-control.***

Printed in Great Britain
by Amazon